Radicalisation and Terrorism:

A Teacher's Handbook for Addressing Extremism

Alison Jamieson
Jane Flint

Brilliant
PUBLICATIONS

For Mollie, Sophie, Lucy, Eilidh and 'Hamish'

Published by Brilliant Publications
Unit 10
Sparrow Hall Farm
Edlesborough
Dunstable
Bedfordshire
LU6 2ES, UK

www.brilliantpublications.co.uk

The name Brilliant Publications and the logo are registered trademarks.

Written by Alison Jamieson and Jane Flint
Preface by Conor Gearty
Edited by Marie Birkinshaw
Illustrations by Kerry Ingham
Picture researcher: Susannah Jayes, Mayflower Media Ltd
Thank you to the following people/organisations for granting us permission to use their photographs on our cover:
top left: © Reuters/Corbis
top right: © Walter Dhladhla/AFP/Getty Images
middle left: © Danish Siddiqui/Reuters/Corbis
middle right: © Rex Features Ltd
bottom left: © Georges Gobet/AFP/Getty Images
bottom right: © Monkey Business Images/Shutterstock Inc

The poem 'If mice could roar' from *Ruskin Bond's Book of Verse*, Penguin Books India (2007) has been reprinted with the generous permission of Ruskin Bond and Penguin Books India.

The poem 'Let no one steal your dreams' has been reprinted with the generous permission of Paul Cookson (2001).

Preface

By Conor Gearty, Director of the Institute of Public Affairs and Professor of Human Rights Law, London School of Economics

Government asks us to be concerned about radicalisation in our schools. We are to beware of extremism, and vigilant against all efforts to use positions of authority to inculcate propaganda into our children. The spectre of terrorism haunts this discussion, hanging over us like some alien virus preparing for a devastating swoop on our young. But what is terrorism? How can we tell 'unacceptable' extremist views from those that evidence instead a healthy classroom debate? If schools are, as the government says, 'ungoverned spaces' is this a social good or a dangerous weakness in the 'arsenal of democracy'? How can teachers (and their pupils) negotiate all this with minimal guidance from the authorities, whose rhetoric may be fine but whose command of detail is often so weak? Alison Jamieson and Jane Flint are doing a vital service for our educators in taking on this subject, at once so topical and so politicised in its reach. Their great learning is distilled into a series of clear propositions which rise above the array of received opinion from our various 'experts' and in so doing produce a pathway leading to greater understanding. The case studies make sense of the vague language of terrorism by giving it a life and meaning by reference to specific historical situations. The media is put in its proper place, a vehicle for the communication of terrorist messages but at times inflamer too of the anxieties which terrorist violence induces. Teachers and pupils will find in this volume learning and guidance that cuts through polemic and overstatement. There is nothing like this available today. No school addressing these issues should be without it.

Contents

Preface 3

Introduction 7

How to Get the Most from this Handbook 11

Definitions, Terminology and Sources 17

Unit 1: Terrorism – What It Is and What It Isn't 22

1.1   Impressions and questionnaire 23

1.2   What IS terrorism? 25

1.3   What ISN'T terrorism? 27

1.4   What do terrorists want? 28

1.5   Unfairness, discrimination and rights 29

1.6   Non-violent protest 31

1.7   Changing things through violence 34

        Storyline: the Riverside Park protest 35

Unit 2: 'Terrorism' and History 40

2.1   Introduction 41

2.2   Assassins, Thugs and Suffragettes 41

2.3   World War 2 and the French Resistance movement 47

2.4   Nelson Mandela 47

2.5   What do they have in common and how are they different? 51

2.6   Terrorism – a universal agreement? 51

Unit 3: The Jigsaw of Terrorism 54

3.1   Introduction 55

        Storyline: Bobo – a narrative of hate 56

3.2   The reasons, or the WHY? of terrorism 59

3.3   The goals, or the WHAT FOR? of terrorism 61

3.4   The methods, or the HOW? of terrorism 62

3.5   The pathways, or the WHAT WAY? into terrorism 64

3.6   Optional case studies 66

Unit 4: Terrorism and the Media 76

4.1   Who are the media and what do they do? 77

4.2   Fact, opinion and bias 79

4.3   Terrorism as performance 81

4.4   The terrorist message 83

	4.5	The media and positive messages	84
	4.6	The media and negative messages	85
	4.7	Reporting on terrorism: finding a balance	87
	4.8	Doing deals with terrorists: the media are involved	91

Unit 5: Pulling It All Together 94

	5.1	Does terrorism ever go away, and how?	95
	5.2	Healing the wounds	98
	5.3	We are all the colours of the rainbow	100
	5.4	Reconciliation and restoring justice – old traditions can help	101
	5.5	Courageous People	103
	5.6	Optional revision discussions	105
	5.7	The problem of 'defining' terrorism	107
	5.8	Final thoughts on terrorism	108

Photocopy Masters	113
Glossary of Key Vocabulary	119
Endnotes	121
Bibliography and Further Reading	123
Suggested Online Resources	124
Acknowledgements	126
Biographical Notes	127

Introduction

In the summer of 2015 when this Handbook went to press, terrorism occupied global news headlines on a daily basis. As the brutality of terrorism is experienced by more communities across more countries, the multiple challenges that it poses have rarely seemed more intractable. Community and school leaders, parents and teachers are expected to contribute to prevention efforts within the framework of government policies that, inevitably, are driven by the need to attain achievable goals in the lifespan of electoral cycles. As regards terrorism, such goals can be elusive. Our approach in writing this book is to take a step back and to take a longer and broader view: to strip terrorism down to its component parts, to look at its origins – in anger, hatred and perceived injustice – and to study the past for insights into the present. We even provide some optimism for the future.

This Handbook provides a reliable and objective resource for classroom use that enables lower secondary school teachers to tackle the complex issues of terrorism, radicalisation and extremism with confidence. It is a teacher-led journey through political violence, viewed in the context of a debate on citizenship, human rights and respect, civil and political engagement and forms of protest.

Teachers can use this Handbook to explain what terrorists do and why they do it; how to differentiate between the *reasons, goals* and *methods* of terrorists; how to explain the complex pathways that lead to involvement in violence; why the media and terrorism are inextricably linked; how and why terrorism starts and, crucially, what factors bring a cycle of terrorism to an end. By stimulating debate, role-play and critical thinking, this text provides a forum for pupils to explore grievances, analyse and put forward moral arguments, consider the nature of protest and its relationship to violence and to engage in wide-ranging discussions of major issues affecting their own and the global community.

Why is this Handbook needed?

This resource text is structured around several premises. The first is that children from the age of 11 will have heard the word 'terrorism' used with some frequency at home, on television and through social media, but have at best a vague understanding of what the term signifies. In the United States since 9/11 and in the UK since the London bombings of July 2005, young people have been aware that something called 'terrorism' is not necessarily a remote event in a far-off country but can happen on their doorstep. Some may have been directly affected by terrorism, or have had friends or family who were. Teenagers across Europe know that hundreds of their peers, some as young as 15, have been recruited to fight alongside terrorist groups in Syria and Iraq, but are confused as to how and why. Terrorism has become one of the most widely used but least understood terms in everyday language.

Secondly, many adults, whether parents or teachers, are also unclear about what terrorism is and find it difficult to respond to questions on the subject from children. There is a great deal of confusion in the public at large as to the meaning of the terms terrorism, extremism and radicalisation, yet there are few resources available that enable the teaching profession to explain these complex and controversial issues in the school classroom, especially to this younger age group.

Thirdly, just as teaching professionals require a reliable and objective resource text to use in classroom discussions, so equally do pupils. Young people are well aware that their habits, interests and online behaviour have become a target for suspicion and scrutiny. In the period from 2007 to March 2014, 153 children under 11, a further 690 aged 12–15 and 554 aged 16–17, primarily from Muslim communities, had been referred to the UK government's *Channel* programme to be assessed for the risk of being drawn into terrorism.[1] Radicalisation and terrorism are problems that school pupils find deeply troubling. They need help to extricate meaning from the confusing terminology, facile slogans and loose jargon that dominate headline-driven news items. What every secondary school should now offer is a debating space, carefully constructed and with impartial leadership, where these important issues are discussed and where pupils' concerns can be addressed.

Fourthly and finally, the UK government has made it imperative to fill this resource gap in the education curriculum. The Counter-Terrorism and Security Act of February 2015 delivered a new range of statutory responsibilities for which many teachers, as well as others within the 'specified authorities' designated under the Act, feel ill prepared. In addition to their regular teaching duties, school staff, governors and leaders are now obliged to 'have due regard to the need to prevent people from being drawn into terrorism' with responsibility to 'establish or use existing mechanisms for understanding the risk of radicalisation.' According to guidelines published in March 2015[2] they 'need to know what measures are available to prevent people from becoming drawn into terrorism and how to challenge the extremist ideology that can be associated with it.' They have a duty to ensure that schools are 'safe places in which children and young people can understand and discuss sensitive topics, including terrorism and the extremist ideas that are part of terrorist ideology, and learn how to challenge these ideas.' After training, teachers should have 'the knowledge and confidence to identify children at risk of being drawn into terrorism and to challenge extremist ideas which can be used to legitimise terrorism and are shared by terrorist groups.' These are onerous responsibilities indeed.

The UK is far from alone in having to face the challenges of youth radicalisation in different forms. Many countries across the world are struggling to protect their young and vulnerable populations and to build up their resistance to extremist narratives based on fear and hatred. The emphasis on Islamist terrorism in western government policy and in public perceptions of violence may have contributed to a neglect of other forms of religious and racial hatred. Since 9/11 white supremacists, anti-government fanatics and other non-Muslim extremists in the US carried out almost twice as many attacks as radical Muslims; right-wing extremism and attacks on religious minorities have grown steadily in many West European countries in the last five years, with at best a lukewarm policy response from national parliaments. This Handbook's wide-ranging geographical coverage ensures its relevance and applicability to educators in other countries seeking a resource book with which to introduce modern conflict studies.

What does this Handbook cover?

The core study area of the Handbook examines the multiple processes that lead to terrorism and the effects of terrorism on individuals and communities. However the approach is indirect, and teachers reach this core from different angles. Entry points include a consideration of familiar violent behaviour such as bullying, a debate on violence and non-violence centred on Mahatma Gandhi and Dr Martin Luther King Jr, and a discussion of the struggle – sometimes violent – for women's rights and universal suffrage led by the Suffragettes. Deriving in each case from a perceived injustice or grievance, the paths converge on the process of engagement in terrorist violence and how perspectives on violence change with time and circumstances. The question of whether former South African president Nelson Mandela was a 'terrorist' or a 'man of peace' is used as illustration.

Violence is inseparable from terrorism, and how terrorists use violence is key to understanding the phenomenon. Individual pathways into terrorism vary widely and may also differ between males and females. The process may be mediated through peers, kinship groups, a powerful or influential communicator, by access to Internet and social media sites preaching violence or, more likely, by a combination of these factors.[3] The decision to engage in violence may evolve gradually from influences absorbed actively or passively over months or years, or may explode in a sudden and imperative need to act. It calls into question the nature of identity, how individuals perceive themselves and the means by which they identify with others. Four widely differing case studies illustrate in greater detail the causes and consequences of terrorism in different regions around the world. Fictional storylines and classroom activities are provided to stimulate critical thinking and interactive participation.

An important Unit of the book introduces the role of the mass media and social networks in terrorism, including in recruitment and propaganda. Pupils reflect on the role that fact, opinion and bias play in media messages, and how misleading or distorted messages can change the way a story is presented. A greater awareness of the risks of bias and media manipulation may encourage pupils to challenge pro-violence messages and to adopt a more critical approach to online source evaluation. While it is never possible to protect pupils entirely from the proselytising effects of violent discourse, teachers can use this text to build resilience and create counter narratives that will strengthen pupils' defences against them.

The last Unit of the Handbook examines the factors that bring a cycle of violence to an end, and introduces the principles of reconciliation and restorative justice. The notion of 'Courageous People' is introduced – those who put their lives and reputations at risk in helping to resolve conflicts. Programmes for the rehabilitation of young fighters from conflict zones are discussed, with possible relevance for the present day. The Unit concludes with brief summaries and questions on what has been learned and (for older classes) tackles the problem of reaching a definition of terrorism, a term which is value-laden and subjective, and about which there is no international consensus.

A classroom questionnaire, distributed at the start and at the end of study, provides a measure of what has been learned.

Does the Handbook reach any conclusions?

History suggests that terrorist violence rarely achieves its goals, and is destructive of both those who practise and those who suffer it. Even if individuals have genuine and unresolved grievances, the use of violence against unarmed civilians (as terrorism is most commonly defined) is more likely to lead to further violence and suffering than to any lasting peaceful solution. The Handbook concludes that terrorism can and does end if there is enough will to do so and if principles of human rights, equality of treatment and fairness before the law are respected. Terrorism is 'man-made' and therefore can be ended by 'man', although peace has a better chance if women are involved in the process.

This Handbook is intended not only as a resource text on radicalisation and terrorism but also as a means to involve classes in a much broader discussion of diversity and identity, conflict resolution and the difficulties of human relations in which everyone, including pupils as young as 11, can participate.

Alison Jamieson
Jane Flint

How to Get the Most from this Handbook

The Handbook has been written in order to support you, the teacher, in your daily work and to give you the confidence to tackle the complex issues of terrorism, radicalisation and extremism serenely and competently. Its aim is to help you not only to fulfil your statutory obligations but also to create an enjoyable and creative classroom environment that will enrich your teaching experience and bring benefits across the entire school curriculum. We hope that in turn your pupils will appreciate the opportunity to debate the issues in a constructive and stimulating way. If we have achieved these aims, we will have succeeded.

We recommend that before beginning your preparation of the lessons you read the next section on *Definitions, Terminology and Sources*. This will help you to find a way through the minefield of confusing terms that relate to terrorist activity, and will better prepare you for tackling the teaching, classroom activities and questions that will follow.

How the Handbook is structured

The Handbook is divided into five **Units**. These Units are written incrementally with a building block effect, such that each Unit builds on a framework of examples and concepts introduced previously, and it is recommended that you follow this order. It will enable you to begin work with simpler ideas with which pupils are familiar – the experiences of anger and disappointment, the notion of fairness and unfairness – and progress gradually to the more complex and nuanced ideas that characterise the subsequent Units.

Unit 1 provides a general introduction to the subject of terrorism with an exploration of types of violence. A list of recent terrorist attacks is provided for your reference. Terrorism is partly explained in terms of what it is not, using examples with which pupils are familiar. Moving on to what terrorism 'is' shows that a number of specific 'ingredients' must be present to call something terrorism. The idea of a terrorism cooking pot is introduced. The answers to a simple questionnaire will give you a sense of what pupils believe about terrorism.

Unit 2 digresses into a historical overview of different kinds of violence which were or might have been called terrorism, and explains why putting the label of terrorism on to violent behaviour is so controversial. In this Unit examples of the Suffragettes and Nelson Mandela are used to illustrate how people's views of violence differ and how they change over time.

Unit 3 goes to the heart of how terrorism evolves and explores different pathways into terrorist violence. A simple Storyline looks at how terrorism affects one individual and his family. The various aspects that we need to know about terrorism are explained as a set of jigsaw sections which we try to assemble into a whole. These sections are called the *reasons*, *goals* and *methods* of terrorism, together with the process of involvement in terrorist activity which we call *pathways*.   >>

The second half of the Unit studies four very different forms of terrorism – from Northern Ireland, Italy, the Middle East and Papua New Guinea – and draws out the essential characteristics of terrorism, how violence developed and how (in three cases) it ended. Pupils are invited to reflect on the consequences of terrorism, and how destructive it is for aggressors as well as victims.

Unit 4 examines the role of the media in terrorism from both positive and negative perspectives. It makes a distinction between *fact, opinion* and *bias*, and encourages role-play and debate on these issues. The Unit shows how terrorists have a message for *victims, target* and *audience*, and how this puts pressure on governments and public opinion. The way in which biased or misleading information is communicated alerts pupils to the need for critical evaluation of information sources, and encourages them to challenge pro-violence messages.

Unit 5 looks at how terrorism ends, with a particular focus on conflict resolution mechanisms and the role of peacemakers. It asks pupils to remember the key points of previous Units and, for older pupils, proposes a definition of terrorism based on what has been learned.

The Handbook concludes that terrorism can and usually does come to an end, particularly when: participants on all sides are weary of violence and see no likelihood of victory; 'Courageous People' are prepared to risk their lives and reputations for peace; laws are fair to all groups in a population; hatred and the desire for revenge can be put aside and former enemies can learn to trust one another.

Curriculum suggestions

With subject matter as sensitive and controversial as terrorism, we suggest that this Handbook is introduced as **part of a whole school strategy**, with head teachers taking ultimate responsibility. Given the new statutory responsibilities that schools have for safeguarding and prevention, it may not be strictly necessary to inform parents and carers about the course of study. However we recommend doing so as a courtesy and to pre-empt objections. For example a letter or policy statement could give notice of the school's intention to adopt the Handbook, giving a brief outline of the course. The letter could explain that the school has new statutory obligations that must be fulfilled; that the course of study will expand the school's core values and principles of human rights, equality, diversity and civic engagement. A brief summary of lesson content could follow, with examples of how these will complement other parts of the curriculum.

We recommend that the Handbook be taught within the **Citizenship** curriculum with which it shares the themes of human rights and democratic values, equality of race, religion and gender and participation in civil society. The current Citizenship curriculum gives particular emphasis to Britain and British values (about which we have reservations – see *Definitions, Terminology and Sources*) but it also requires teaching to 'equip pupils with the skills and knowledge to explore political and social issues critically, to weigh evidence, debate and make reasoned arguments.' In this light we think that the Handbook makes an excellent fit with Citizenship. Several sections of the Handbook, particularly in Unit 2, could usefully be studied within or alongside the KS3 **History** curriculum. For example, within the History module 'Ideas, political power, industry and empire: Britain 1745–1901', a study of the British empire with a focus on India would tie in well with our study of Indian independence leader Mahatma Gandhi; the module, 'Challenges for Britain, Europe and the wider world 1901 to the present day' would link up well with our study of the Suffragettes. There is also an overlap with **RE** which could stimulate fruitful discussions. **PSHE** has two thematic areas of relevance to this Handbook: 'Relationships', and 'Living in the Wider World'. Ideally, teaching staff from all four disciplines would consult on coordinating lesson plans. Proceeding on this basis should enrich and complement studies across the curriculum.

What to look out for in each Unit

Brief introductory summary

Key skills developed in each Unit

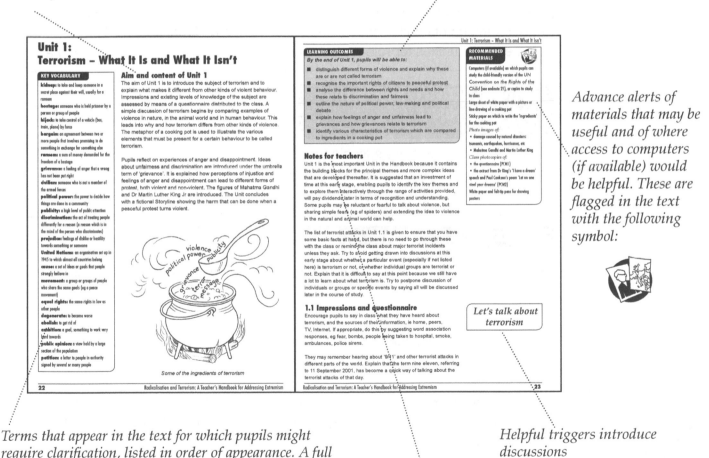

Advance alerts of materials that may be useful and of where access to computers (if available) would be helpful. These are flagged in the text with the following symbol:

Terms that appear in the text for which pupils might require clarification, listed in order of appearance. A full easy-reference alphabetic glossary appears at the end of the Handbook

Helpful triggers introduce discussions

Practical aspects for introducing the Units and highlights of problematic or sensitive issues that might need to be dealt with

Other special features and symbols used

CLASSROOM/ASSEMBLY ACTIVITY

Classroom/assembly activities are a core element of this text, and we recommend that you always make time for them. In general the activities are grouped at the end of a section and serve to recap on what has been covered, with a focus on summing up what has been learned in the section. Occasionally activities are suggested during discussion of a specific issue. These serve to lighten up what might otherwise be a particularly dense discussion. They also allow pupils' feelings on a particular issue to be given immediate expression before they pass or are forgotten.

The classroom activities are important because they broaden the range of a discussion, stimulating pupils to work out and articulate views on issues that are related to but not confined to violence. They encourage pupils to explore the nature of conflict and grievance and to seek non-violent solutions to problems in their own lives and in the wider world. They invite pupils to test themselves against the moral arguments for and against the use of violence and to relate their own understanding of conflict and its consequences to a global sphere. They provide ample opportunities for role-play, drama and debate at all levels of age and ability.

OPTIONAL ACTIVITY/INFORMATION FOR OLDER PUPILS

While most activities are suitable for all KS3 age groups, these are more suitable for older pupils. If you prefer to skip these older age options, you are invited to pass directly to the next appropriate section as indicated.

SUMMARY

Helpful summary points to conclude each Unit to ensure key learning has been achieved.

PCM

This symbol indicates the availability of handy photocopiable sheets printed at the end of the Handbook.

These 'Tip' pointers suggest how you can illustrate a particular theme or encourage the class to respond in a particular way.

Two fictional **STORYLINES** are used to illustrate key themes of the Handbook. The Unit 1 Storyline describes what happens to a peaceful protest movement when violence is used; the Unit 3 Storyline portrays an individual's pathway into violence, with the consequences of that choice. The Unit 3 Storyline can be used for younger pupils as an alternative to the four case studies in the final part of Unit 3.

Two pieces of **POETRY** are included in the text: the first, by Paul Cookson, follows Dr Martin Luther King Jr's 'I have a dream' speech and encourages pupils not to give up their ambitions. The second, by Anglo-Indian poet Ruskin Bond, concludes the Handbook with a light-hearted vision of what a better world might look like.

Guidelines for classroom discussions

Your success in using this Handbook will depend on the extent to which you encourage lively debate and dialogue between you and your pupils, and between pupils themselves. Before embarking on a lesson we recommend you think through carefully your own position and feelings on the issues to be discussed, being aware of any bias you might have. Don't be afraid to give opinions but if possible avoid stating these as facts or absolutes. Try not to draw conclusions or make definitive statements unless these are well-rehearsed or approved school policies such as respect for human rights, gender and racial equality, etc. Terrorism and radicalisation are topics which lend themselves too easily to generalisation and broad sweeping statements. Reaching a tentative conclusion and leaving space for doubt is better than pretending to have a definitive answer to a problem. Accepting the absence of certainty should not, for the purposes of this Handbook, be construed as something negative. Because terrorism has no accepted universal definition then there will always be room for subjectivity, disagreement and doubt. If you are faced with difficult questions, do not feel the need to respond immediately. You can always postpone an answer until you have discussed it with colleagues or your school leadership team. Simply comment that you need some time to think before replying. The PSHE Association guidelines on these issues can be helpful here.[4]

Despite the seriousness of the subject matter, try to keep the lessons light-hearted and enjoyable. Avoid excessive focus on extreme Islamist groups, bearing in mind the broad spectrum of political violence that is covered in this Handbook and the centuries that it spans. Do not allow these lessons to be used or perceived as a means of assessing pupils for their potential to radicalisation, as any impression that pupils feel themselves 'under surveillance' will inhibit discussion and stifle debate. It goes without saying, however, that if any pupils give specific indications that they risk being drawn into terrorism then you must follow your school's policy in this regard.

Classroom discussions should be conducted in a democratic fashion and according to rules that you must set. Each pupil should be allowed a voice, and dialogue should be encouraged. Digressions from the major themes into local or community issues should be allowed, though not to the detriment of the major themes. You may already have a set of guidelines for conducting classroom debate and if they have worked well you should retain them.

Here are a few tips which may help with controversial issues dealt with in this Handbook:

■ Once you have set up a debate and its rules, encourage the class to set the pace. You may be the moderator or you may prefer to appoint a pupil moderator who will take views and summarise the arguments. With some classes you could adopt the role of devil's advocate or appoint a pupil to the role.

■ One pupil should speak at a time for a limited number of minutes with no interrupting allowed.

■ Pupils' views must be listened to but if their expressed opinions contradict the school's values or the values of a democratic society (tolerance, equality of human rights, etc) they must be challenged firmly, preferably with the moderator asking other pupils to provide counter arguments.

■ Hate speech, racism, religious or sexist comments should be challenged with examples of their consequences, eg the Holocaust, apartheid.

■ Encourage pupils to challenge ideas rather than people.

■ Be aware of the possibility that pupils are repeating parrot fashion what they may have heard or read. To counter this, encourage pupils with outspoken views to justify them.

■ Do not confuse the desire to 'be different', to brag or to shock with a genuine sympathy for terrorism. Deliberate provocation should be dealt with firmly.

■ Some of the issues lend themselves well to drama and role-play, and these should be encouraged as alternatives to debate.

Lesson planning

We have not included detailed lesson plans nor have we tried to estimate how long you should devote to each Unit or section, as these will depend on the ability and age group of your classes and the curriculum time available. Do not rush the lessons, it is better to cover one section carefully if the pupils are stimulated than trying to cover several sections superficially. We suggest that the course of study should range from a minimum of one term to a maximum of one school year. You may find it helpful to use a Progress Chart as a guide to arranging and planning lessons and to help future users of the Handbook.

An example:

Date	Class	Material covered	Activities	Time taken	Comments
19/10/2015	Y7	Unit 1: 1.1–1.5	Questionnaire and class discussion on terrorism	40 mins	Most of class seemed familiar with key vocabulary. Some personal fears over terrorist attacks. High participation in class discussions; seemed to find lesson useful.

Definitions, Terminology and Sources

This text draws on scholarly research to analyse and interpret the origins and rationale of terrorism, in particular the work of Amartya Sen, Conor Gearty, John Horgan, Richard English, Bruce Hoffman and Louise Richardson. Professor Lynn Davies' book, *Educating Against Extremism*[5], has also been a valuable guide in identifying educational approaches to combating extremism.

Definitions

The range of definitions of terrorism used by scholars and governments is extensive and can be consulted in the texts cited. Bruce Hoffman[6] defines terrorism as

> *the deliberate creation and exploitation of fear through violence or the threat of violence in the pursuit of political change.*

Conor Gearty[7] states

> *Violence is unequivocally terrorist when it is politically motivated and carried out by sub-state groups; when its victims are chosen at random; and when the purpose behind the violence is to communicate a message to a wider audience.*

Section 1 of the UK Terrorism Act 2000[8] defines terrorism as

> *the use or threat of action made for the purpose of advancing a political, religious, racial or ideological cause where the use or threat is designed to influence the government or an international governmental organisation or to intimidate the public or a section of the public.*

This occurs when the action

> *(a) involves serious violence against a person,*
> *(b) involves serious damage to property,*
> *(c) endangers a person's life, other than that of the person committing the action,*
> *(d) creates a serious risk to the health or safety of the public or a section of the public, or*   >>

> *(e) is designed seriously to interfere with or seriously to disrupt an electronic system.*

We try to build up a composite picture of terrorism in the course of the Handbook, beginning with the simple notion of a cooking pot containing a number of ingredients without which we cannot call something 'terrorism'. In later Units the negative labelling of the term and the problems of subjectivity are explained. We describe the various aspects that we need to know about terrorism as sections of a jigsaw puzzle to be assembled. These include *reasons, goals* and *methods*, which may be common and shared by many, as well as *pathways* into terrorism which are unique to each individual.

At the end of the book we propose a simple definition using terms with which pupils have become familiar during their study:

> *Terrorism is deliberate violence or the threat of violence for political goals, usually by non-state individuals or groups, against a civilian population. It is used to cause terror and to send a message to a wider audience, and aims to force a section of the population, an authority or a government to change its behaviour.*

The word political is used here in its broadest sense to include the power to decide the rules by which a community lives, including religious practices. Pupils are encouraged to modify or build on this definition.

We explain the phenomenon of terrorism as a form of warfare, usually carried out by 'non-state' individuals or groups, ie who are not acting on behalf of a country or a state. However we also acknowledge that governments have used 'state' terrorism as a tool of their domestic and/or foreign policies (see p 50).

The difficulty of finding a universally accepted definition of terrorism is discussed at various points in the Handbook, and the 14 UN Conventions[9] on terrorist acts are introduced in Unit 3.4. An important obstacle to finding a universal definition is that countries cannot agree on the distinction between acts of terrorism and acts carried out as part of a legitimate struggle for self-determination and liberation from foreign, colonial or alien occupation. The latter are recognised as legal under the United Nations charter. There is also disagreement over whether acts involving armed forces personnel can be described as terrorist. The 14 UN Conventions do not cover acts of violence involving members of the armed forces because (a) 'conventional' warfare sometimes involves military attacks on civilians or civilian structures and (b) there is no agreement on whether attacks on military personnel in non-combat situations – that is when they are off-duty and unarmed – should be called terrorism.

Confusing terminology

Other terms discussed in this Handbook are *extreme* and *extremism, radical* and *radicalisation*. These words are open to different interpretations. Radicalisation is defined in the UK government's *Prevent* strategy 2011[10] as 'the process by which a person comes to support terrorism and forms of extremism leading to terrorism.' Violent extremism, according to *Prevent*, is 'the endorsement of violence to achieve extreme ends.' Extremism is defined as 'vocal or active opposition to fundamental British values, including democracy, the rule of law, individual liberty and mutual respect and tolerance of different faiths and beliefs.'

Our interpretation of extremism differs slightly. Whilst we agree that these values are British and are of paramount importance, we believe that they have a broader, universal significance that extends beyond British nationality and culture. Nor do we make any assumptions that radicalisation leads inexorably to 'extreme ends'. We suggest that extreme or radical views are those which are not shared by the majority of the population but that having such views does not indicate that an individual supports or participates in violent activity. We suggest that the process of radicalisation can be understood in terms of a movement towards a position where the use of violence appears acceptable or desirable, and that an individual who has been radicalised may support or participate in terrorist acts. We try wherever possible to avoid absolutes, as individual attitudes to violence are not static but extremely fluid, and will vary according to the stage and degree of involvement (or not) in a terrorist group of the individual concerned.

Motivation

Scholarly research, together with my own extensive experience in interviewing Italian left-wing terrorists, has shown that there is nothing inevitable, or immutable, about participation in terrorism nor is there a 'conveyor belt' that leads automatically from grievance to violence. As we try to show, an individual's pathway into terrorism is a uniquely personal choice, bound up with the expectation of a collective benefit that extends to a wider community or group, and one which is nearly always driven by contact with others. To quote Louise Richardson[11], it depends upon a 'lethal cocktail containing a disaffected individual, an enabling community and a legitimising ideology.' It is the coming together of all three that creates the conditions for terrorism to occur.

The importance of grievance in terrorist motivation is stressed in the academic literature.

As John Horgan[12] observes, grievances may be

> *virtual, imaginary or historical'* and *'are often susceptible to change between the onset of terrorist violence and various stages of its subsequent development.*

According to Lord Alderdice[13], psychiatrist and former Speaker of the Northern Ireland Assembly who played a key role in the 1998 Good Friday agreement:

> *The set of thoughts and feelings that has impressed me as most significant in generating violence has to do with experiences of disrespect and humiliation[…] Where individuals and communities are despised and humiliated a bitter sense of injustice is stored up and an almost unquenchable desire develops for vengeance and the righting of wrong.*

Richardson reinforces this idea, suggesting that above all terrorists seek 'revenge, renown and reaction.'[14]

The image that terrorists have of themselves primarily as victims provoked to violence as a result of humiliation or violence inflicted upon them or upon those with whom they identify is common. Militants from Western Europe have been recruited to extremist Islamist organisations in the aftermath of attacks on villages in Afghanistan carried out by the US or its allies, or on learning of humiliation and torture practices against Muslims in Guantanamo Bay and in Abu Ghraib prison in Iraq. It has been suggested that the IRA's surge in recruitment from 1969 was attributable to brutal and humiliating treatment of the Catholic population at the hands of the British security forces from 1969 to the early 1970s and to the policy of internment without trial introduced by the Stormont government in 1971.[15] One of the London suicide bombers of 7 July 2005, Mohammad Siddique Khan, said in a pre-recorded video that his action was in revenge for atrocities against 'his people' in Afghanistan and Iraq. In my interviews with Italian Red Brigadists, motivation was invariably explained in terms of a response to violence inflicted by the state, either directly against student protesters and industrial workers or indirectly through the perceived collusion of state authorities in right-wing bomb attacks.[16] The four case studies used in Unit 3 all reflect the notion of terrorism not merely as ideologically driven but also as arising from feelings of oppression by an enemy whose propensity to use violence has been established, perhaps intensified. Frequently added to this is a sense of the impotence of conventional political channels to effect radical change. For those who take up terrorist violence it is the enemy authority that has been radicalised to violence, and they who must resist.

Terrorist personality

Contrary to popular belief, academic research has shown that most terrorists are not mentally disturbed nor are they psychologically exceptional individuals. Attempts to draw up a typical terrorist 'profile' have generally been unsuccessful. An in-depth study, carried out by the British security service MI5 and seen by *The Guardian* newspaper, of several hundred individuals 'known to be involved in, or closely associated with, violent extremist activity' ranging from fundraising to planning suicide bombings in Britain, concluded that it was not possible to create a profile of the typical British terrorist and that there was 'no single pathway to extremism.'

All those studied 'had taken strikingly different journeys to violent extremist activity', most were 'demographically unremarkable and simply reflect the communities in which they live.'[17] It is sometimes assumed that terrorism against western targets has its origins in a civilisational clash between fanatical Islam on one side and the liberalism of western democracies on the other. Again, scholarly research does not substantiate this claim. As Richard English[18] has observed, terrorism may occur when there are 'competing demands upon the individual of rival cultures', a form of 'cultural ambiguity' that, for example, characterised the group of London bombers. We also suggest in this Handbook that religion may be a component but that it is not usually the principal driver of terrorism, which derives as much from historical and geopolitical grievances as from religious ideology or doctrine. To give excessive attention to religious identity, as has been a recent tendency in Western Europe, ignores multiple aspects of communal identity that exist independently of religious affiliation. To quote Amartya Sen[19], explaining social identity by means of 'faith-based separatism' is not only misleading but encourages the 'purposeful exploitation of divisiveness' that undermines efforts to strengthen community cohesion and a sense of shared citizenship.

Exit strategies

The noble ambitions of reconciliation and respect urged by peacemakers Dr Desmond Tutu and Lord Alderdice that inspire Unit 5 of this Handbook are hard to envisage in the current conflict with Islamic State/ISIS. But with cohorts of young men and women leaving western countries to join the jihadist struggle in Syria and Iraq, we cannot afford to give up. Italy, with its long experience of terrorism and organised criminality, has shown that providing pathways out of terrorism for militants who renounce violence can be a successful strategy. The younger the combatants, the more ready they may be to look for an exit route when expectations of heroic activity clash with the reality of violence given and received. Over time, Italian terrorists facing the prospect of either death in gunfights with police or lengthy imprisonment found their commitment to the cause and to their companions weakening, with 'an onward movement that was sacrificial because we were incapable of finding a way out.'[20] Elements that might constitute a viable strategy for the future could include helping disaffected combatants to return home and disengage from terrorism, with support for communities and families; a legislative framework that favours the renunciation of violence; and the recruitment of former fighters as agents in prevention efforts. First-hand experiences of terrorism that demythologise violence provide a powerful counter narrative. Such policies, if adopted by western governments, might prevent young militants from being trapped in perpetuating cycles of violence.

Alison Jamieson

Unit 1:
Terrorism – What It Is and What It Isn't

KEY VOCABULARY

kidnap: to take and keep someone in a secret place against their will, usually for a ransom

hostage: someone who is held prisoner by a person or group of people

hijack: to take control of a vehicle (bus, train, plane) by force

bargain: an agreement between two or more people that involves promising to do something in exchange for something else

ransom: a sum of money demanded for the freedom of a hostage

grievance: a feeling of anger that a wrong has not been put right

civilian: someone who is not a member of the armed forces

political power: the power to decide how things are done in a community

publicity: a high level of public attention

discrimination: the act of treating people differently for a reason (a reason which is in the mind of the person who discriminates)

prejudice: feelings of dislike or hostility towards something or someone

United Nations: an organisation set up in 1945 to which almost all countries belong

cause: a set of ideas or goals that people strongly believe in

movement: a group or groups of people who share the same goals (eg a peace movement)

equal rights: the same rights in law as other people

degenerate: to become worse

abolish: to get rid of

ambition: a goal, something to work very hard towards

public opinion: a view held by a large section of the population

petition: a letter to people in authority signed by several or many people

Aim and content of Unit 1

The aim of Unit 1 is to introduce the subject of terrorism and to explain what makes it different from other kinds of violent behaviour. Impressions and existing levels of knowledge of the subject are assessed by means of a questionnaire distributed to the class. A simple discussion of terrorism begins by comparing examples of violence in nature, in the animal world and in human behaviour. This leads into why and how terrorism differs from other kinds of violence. The metaphor of a cooking pot is used to illustrate the various elements that must be present for a certain behaviour to be called terrorism.

Pupils reflect on experiences of anger and disappointment. Ideas about unfairness and discrimination are introduced under the umbrella term of 'grievance'. It is explained how perceptions of injustice and feelings of anger and disappointment can lead to different forms of protest, both violent and non-violent. The figures of Mahatma Gandhi and Dr Martin Luther King Jr are introduced. The Unit concludes with a fictional Storyline showing the harm that can be done when a peaceful protest turns violent.

Some of the ingredients of terrorism

LEARNING OUTCOMES

By the end of Unit 1, pupils will be able to:

■ distinguish different forms of violence and explain why these are or are not called terrorism

■ recognise the important rights of citizens to peaceful protest

■ analyse the difference between rights and needs and how these relate to discrimination and fairness

■ outline the nature of political power, law-making and political debate

■ explain how feelings of anger and unfairness lead to grievances and how grievances relate to terrorism

■ identify various characteristics of terrorism which are compared to ingredients in a cooking pot

RECOMMENDED MATERIALS

Computers (if available) on which pupils can study the child-friendly version of the *UN Convention on the Rights of the Child* (see endnote 21), or copies to study in class

Large sheet of white paper with a picture or line drawing of a cooking pot

Sticky paper on which to write the 'ingredients' for the cooking pot

Photo images of:

• damage caused by natural disasters: tsunamis, earthquakes, hurricanes, etc

• Mahatma Gandhi and Martin Luther King

Class photocopies of:

• the questionnaire (PCM1)

• the extract from Dr King's 'I have a dream' speech and Paul Cookson's poem 'Let no one steal your dreams' (PCM2)

White paper and felt-tip pens for drawing posters

Notes for teachers

Unit 1 is the most important Unit in the Handbook because it contains the building blocks for the principal themes and more complex ideas that are developed thereafter. It is suggested that an investment of time at this early stage, enabling pupils to identify the key themes and to explore them interactively through the range of activities provided, will pay dividends later in terms of recognition and understanding. Some pupils may be reluctant or fearful to talk about violence, but sharing simple fears (eg of spiders) and extending the idea to violence in the natural and animal world can help.

The list of terrorist attacks in Unit 1.1 is given to ensure that you have some basic facts at hand, but there is no need to go through these with the class or remind the class about major terrorist incidents unless they ask. Try to avoid getting drawn into discussions at this early stage about whether a particular event (especially if not listed here) is terrorism or not, or whether individual groups are terrorist or not. Explain that it is difficult to say at this point because we still have a lot to learn about what terrorism is. Try to postpone discussion of individuals or groups or specific events by saying all will be discussed later in the course of study.

1.1 Impressions and questionnaire

Encourage pupils to say in class what they have heard about terrorism, and the sources of their information, ie home, peers, TV, Internet. If appropriate, do this by suggesting word association responses, eg fear, bombs, people being taken to hospital, smoke, ambulances, police sirens.

They may remember hearing about '9/11' and other terrorist attacks in different parts of the world. Explain that the term nine eleven, referring to 11 September 2001, has become a quick way of talking about the terrorist attacks of that day.

Let's talk about terrorism

Among the attacks that pupils may know of, depending on where they live, are:

7 August 1998: Truck bombs explode at the US Embassies in Nairobi, Kenya and Dar es Salaam, Tanzania. In Nairobi, 213 are killed, at least 4,000 injured. In Dar es Salaam, 11 are killed, at least 85 wounded.

11 September 2001: Four planes are hijacked after take-off from airports in the eastern United States. Two are crashed into the Twin Towers of the World Trade Center in New York's financial district, one into the US Defense Department in the Pentagon building, Washington DC, one crashes into a field in Pennsylvania. Approximately 3,000 people are killed.

12 October 2002: Three bombs are detonated in or near nightclubs on the island of Bali, Indonesia. 202 are killed, around 209 are injured.

7 July 2005: Suicide bombers detonate bombs on three underground trains and one bus in London during the morning rush hour. As well as the four bombers, 52 are killed, around 700 injured.

26–29 November 2008: In Mumbai, India, 175 people are killed and over 300 injured during a series of shooting and bombing attacks in different parts of the city.

22 July 2011: Anders Breivik, a 32-year-old Norwegian man, detonates a car bomb outside government buildings in Oslo, killing 8 people. He then crosses to Utøya island, 25 miles from Oslo, where he guns down a further 69 people, mostly teenagers, attending a youth camp on the island run by the ruling Labour party. He claims at his trial that left-wing parties in Europe are destroying the continent's Christian heritage by allowing mass Muslim immigration.

9 October 2012: Malala Yousafzai, a 15-year-old Pakistani schoolgirl, is shot three times by a Taliban gunman as she boards her school bus in Pakistan's Swat valley. She has written and spoken out against the cruel practices of the Taliban, who controlled the valley for two years and who decreed that girls should not go to school.

22 May 2013: Drummer Lee Rigby of the Royal Regiment of Fusiliers is hacked to death while off-duty near the Royal Artillery Barracks in Woolwich, south London. His attackers, two British men raised as Christians but converted to Islam, said they wanted to avenge the murders of Muslims by British soldiers. In the following 5 days 10 attacks are carried out against mosques and hundreds of threats made against British Muslims.

14 April 2014: 276 girls, mostly Christian, are kidnapped from their boarding school in northern Nigeria by the group Boko Haram, whose name means 'western education is forbidden'.

August–October 2014: Two US journalists, James Foley and Steven Sotloff and two British aid workers, David Haines and Alan Henning, kidnapped in Syria by Islamic State/ISIS, are brutally murdered, apparently by a man with an English accent.

16 December 2014: 7 Taliban gunmen attack an army-run school in Peshawar, Pakistan, killing 141 people, 132 of them children. A Taliban spokesman said the attack was punishment for Pakistani army operations against the Taliban.

7 January 2015: Two brothers, Chérif and Saïd Kouachi, attack the offices of the magazine *Charlie Hebdo* in central Paris, killing 12 people, including two police officers. Two days later, as French special forces surround them in a warehouse north of Paris, another gunman, Amedy Coulibaly, takes 19 people hostage in a Jewish supermarket in Paris. He threatens to kill them unless the Kouachis are allowed to go free. The Kouachis are killed in a gunfight. Coulibaly shoots four hostages before being killed by police. The Kouachi brothers claimed they belonged to Al-Qaeda, Coulibaly to Islamic State.

18 March 2015: Three gunmen take hostage a group of foreign tourists as they leave their tour bus to visit the Bardo museum in Tunis, Tunisia. They shoot dead 21 tourists and a Tunisian policeman, and injure 50 more. The attack is claimed by Islamic State/ISIS. Days later tens of thousands of Tunisians take to the streets to protest against terrorism and to demonstrate their belief in Tunisia's democracy.

A terrorist attack may have affected the friends or families of pupils in the class. Ask them if they know or know of anyone who has been caught up in a terrorist attack. What did that person think/feel? What did the pupil think/feel about it?

Introduce the questionnaire (PCM1) and ask pupils to complete it either verbally in class, or by dividing into groups and writing down their answers. Ask them to give reasons for their answers where possible. Do not pass comment or criticise at this stage, but afterwards summarise with the class the most frequent and significant aspects of their responses. Keep the answers and repeat the questionnaire once you reach the end of the Handbook. The second set of answers should vary considerably from the first.

PCM1

1.2 What IS terrorism?

Explain that, although we hear the word terrorism used quite a lot, and we think we recognise it when we read about it or watch TV, it is quite difficult to say what terrorism actually *is*. Ask pupils to think of terrorism as a cooking pot in which there are a certain number of ingredients. Unless these ingredients are in the pot we should not call it terrorism.

Start with the basics:
Explain that the very word 'terrorism' tells us the first thing about it: it causes terror. Ask pupils to find other words similar to 'terror', eg fear, panic. Ask pupils to take it in turns to say 'People are frightened when ...' or, 'People are terrorised by ...' Or start the ball rolling yourself by saying, 'I am very frightened of ... wasps/spiders/snakes/sudden loud noises ...'

If appropriate, gently encourage pupils to talk about any other, more serious or distressing experiences of fear they may have had. Alternatively, ask the class to mime, or make a drawing of someone who is very frightened by another person or by a situation.

Explain that there are lots of different kinds of violence in the world. Violence can be caused by humans, by animals or by nature. Talk about and/or show pictures of damage done by an earthquake, a flood, a tsunami or a hurricane. These events are violent and they cause great harm to people and buildings. We call them 'extreme' events or 'natural disasters' when they happen in nature. Terrorism doesn't happen in nature, it is 'man-made'. Terrorism takes people by

surprise, like an earthquake does. But the people who cause terrorism – we call them terrorists – plan their attacks carefully, sometimes for weeks, months or even years.

Terrorist violence can take many different forms. Often these involve gun or bomb attacks on buildings and on people, who are killed or injured. Terrorists don't always use violence, sometimes they just threaten to do so. Discuss the word *threat*. Ask pupils to stand in pairs. One should take up a 'threatening' position against the other.

Terrorists sometimes **kidnap** people – this means they take them away to a secret place and hide them there. The people they kidnap are called **hostages**.

Hijacking is another method used by terrorists, and involves taking over a vehicle. Terrorists force the driver of a bus to go somewhere he doesn't want to, or the pilot of a plane to fly to another country. When they get there, the terrorists hold the driver or pilot and all the passengers as hostages. It's not a secret place, everyone knows where they are. But if the government tries to rescue the hostages, there is a risk that the terrorists may kill them.

Explain that when terrorists carry out a hijacking or a kidnapping they often want something in exchange for letting the hostages go. They want to make a **bargain** with the people in charge, often the government. The bargain might be, 'We will let the hostages go if you free members of our group from jail.' Or the terrorists may want money. The money paid to free a hostage is called a **ransom**. They threaten to kill the hostages – and sometimes they do – if they don't get what they want. So even if terrorists do not actually hurt people, they are always ready to use violence.

Invite pupils to think of an everyday example of something they think is unfair. For example ask them to imagine that their little brother/sister has taken their favourite toy, game or book (or other favourite item) and badly damaged it. Ask them how they would feel when they saw the damaged book/game/toy. What would they do next?

Ask them now to imagine very strong feelings of anger – lasting years or even generations – that a wrong hasn't been put right. Add to these feelings a sense that there is no hope of things ever improving. The result is what we call **grievances**. Sometimes grievances are real and come from unfair treatment, at other times they may be exaggerated or invented. Whenever we find terrorism we find people with strong grievances.

Explain to pupils that in themselves grievances are not enough to trigger terrorism. Many people feel angry and unhappy, that things

> *Terrorism is the use or threat of violence to cause terror*

Suggest that they would feel angry, and would protest about what has happened to an adult or carer. Discuss the expectation that the wrong would be put right. Ask pupils how they would feel if it wasn't put right. They would be *angry* and *disappointed*, and feel very strongly that things were unfair.

> *Terrorism involves strong feelings of anger and disappointment that a wrong has not been put right. These feelings are called grievances*

are unfair and that they have been treated badly, but they don't use violence. Terrorists always have grievances, but they also need an enemy to hate. The enemy is the authority or people in charge who are blamed for all the things that seem to be unfair.

> *Terrorists want to take revenge on a hated enemy*

Explain that the victims of terrorism – those who are injured or killed in a terrorist attack – are usually ordinary people going about their daily lives – walking round shops or a market, going to work on a bus or train, travelling on a plane. These people are just there by chance, they are not armed but are ordinary **civilians**. For terrorists, they are not the main enemy. The people in charge of things, like important politicians, are the enemy. Political leaders are usually civilians too but they have bodyguards and are protected. They live in houses with high walls away from everyone else. Ordinary people don't have bodyguards, so it is easier to attack them. Terrorists know that after an attack in a crowded place or on public transport, people may be frightened to go on planes or buses, or to go to markets and shopping malls. Somehow they don't feel as safe as they did before. That is exactly what terrorists want.

> *The victims of terrorism are* *usually* **ordinary people**

1.3 What ISN'T terrorism?

Explain that it can help us to understand what terrorism is by knowing what it isn't. Some kinds of violence don't belong in the terrorism cooking pot.

Ask pupils about different kinds of violence in the animal world. Examples could include a lion stalking a zebra or a cat chasing and killing a mouse. Explain that these are NOT terrorism. The cat is doing what cats do naturally, chasing a mouse. The lion must kill in order to live and provide food for its family. But a lion isn't a terrorist. It doesn't sit under a tree making plans to go out and kill a zebra next Friday morning because it hates zebras; it kills because it is hungry and it has to find food or die. So even if cats and lions 'terrorise' other animals, we don't call it terrorism.

Move the discussion to human violence. Ask the class why human beings use violence. Encourage them to answer that people use violence for a purpose. They want a reward from using violence, just like animals do. But the reward is not usually something to eat. Turn the discussion to a form of human violence with which pupils may be familiar: bullying. Discuss bullying with the class, and why it happens.

Ask them if they think bullying has anything in common with terrorism. (We talk about victims of bullying and victims of terrorism.)

Discuss with the class whether someone can use bullying behaviour without actually hurting anyone. Remind them of the saying, 'sticks

and stones may break your bones but names will never harm you.'
Ask if they think that is true, and why/why not.

Give the example of an older pupil waiting for a younger child outside
school. The pupil threatens to beat up the younger child unless the
child gives him some money, or something the child has that the older
pupil wants.

Explain that people who use bullying behaviour have three things in
common with terrorists: they frighten people; they may use or threaten
to use violence; they want a reward. But people who bully are very
different from terrorists. They are often quite lonely individuals who
have had a lot of problems in their own lives. They try to make up for
their own problems by having power over someone else. Terrorists
want different things.

Move on to another example: a bank robber. Give the example of a
bank robber with a gun and a mask over his face who goes into a
bank. He says to all the customers and staff, 'Hands up, don't move
or I'll shoot!' Then he orders a member of the bank staff to hand over
packets of money across the counter. He puts the money in a bag,
runs out of the bank, jumps into a car and drives away.

Is the bank robber using violence, or the threat of violence?
Are the people in the bank terrorised?
Is this terrorism?
Why does someone rob a bank?
What will the bank robber do with the money he takes?
Do you think that bank robbers have anything in common with bullies?
Or with terrorists? What's the difference?

Explain that in some ways a bank robbery is like terrorism: the
customers and staff in the bank are *terrorised*; the bank robber
threatened to use violence; the people in the bank were just *ordinary
people* who happened to be there by chance.

Explain that bank robbers are not terrorists either. Ask the class what
the bank robber will do with the money. The bank robber just wants to
have the money so that he can take it away and spend it. He is selfish
and wants to keep the reward for himself.

> *Terrorists want a reward for
> themselves* and *other people*

1.4 What do terrorists want?

Explain that terrorists want a reward too. But unlike bank robbers, who
want to keep what they win for themselves, terrorists want a reward
for a much larger group of people. We call these rewards *goals*.
Sometimes they want money, because terrorists need money to pay
for weapons and explosives; they need money to rent houses to live

in, and to travel. But they don't spend it on luxury things like fast cars and expensive clothes.

What terrorists most want to win is more difficult to understand – it's what we call **political power**. Explain that having political power means having the right to decide how things are done in a particular community or society without other people interfering. Of course, you can want political power without being a terrorist! The difference is that terrorists threaten or use extreme violence to try to win political power from someone else.

> Don't spend too much time discussing political power at this stage. It will become clearer by the end of the Unit. The point to make is, terrorists don't just want to win a reward or goal for themselves, they want it for other people too.

Terrorists want people to pay attention. Discuss the idea of 'paying attention' in a school context. When the whole class pays attention, everyone listens to what a teacher says. Terrorists want everyone to pay attention, but in a different way. They know that if they kill a famous person, destroy a famous building, or cause an attack in which hundreds of people die then everyone will sit up and pay attention. Televisions all around the world will show what has happened. People will ask themselves why the attack has happened and who the attackers are. Terrorists want as much public attention as possible. This is the same as saying they want **publicity**.

> *Terrorists want people to pay attention*

Explain that there is another reason why bank robbers are not terrorists. They only want to frighten people for a short time while they carry out the robbery. They don't hate the bank staff nor do they want to take revenge on them. Terrorists are different – when they carry out an attack they are using violence to send a *message*. The message is not just for the people who are caught up in the attack but for a bigger or *wider audience*. The message is usually for an authority like a government or other important people. This is the *enemy* whom the terrorists blame for all the bad things they say have happened. The message says, 'We are angry because … This attack was to punish you and we threaten you with more violence if you don't change your behaviour and do what we want.'

> *Terrorists want to send a message and change behaviour*

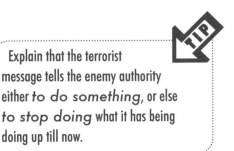

> Explain that the terrorist message tells the enemy authority either *to do something*, or else *to stop doing* what it has being doing up till now.

1.5 Unfairness, discrimination and rights

Explain that we sometimes feel things are unfair if other people are treated differently to us. Sometimes boys are allowed more freedom than girls. In some countries boys are encouraged to study, whereas girls are expected to stay at home. If we think that a particular group of people is being treated unfairly or is not given the same rights as another, then we say there is **discrimination**. It means treating people differently for reasons that are in the mind of whoever does the discriminating. It can mean giving boys more rights than girls. But it is a much bigger idea than that. It can also mean that there is a **prejudice** against them. This may consist of treating people differently because of the colour of their skin, their religion, the clothes they wear, the language they speak, or for other reasons. Just occasionally discrimination can be considered a good thing, for example *positive discrimination* can help people to get jobs who have had particular difficulties or handicaps to overcome.

There is an agreement written down by the **United Nations** (UN), an organisation to which almost every country belongs. It is called the *Universal Declaration of Human Rights*. It says that every human being has certain rights that cannot be taken away. The first sentence says, 'All human beings are born free and equal in dignity and rights.'

Discuss this with the class. Remind pupils that *rights* are not the same as *needs*. Ask them what the difference is. For example we need certain things to stay alive. Discuss with pupils what our essential needs are, ie food, water, clothing and a roof over our heads. This is not true of rights. We don't die because we are not treated the same as other people, but we have reason to be very unhappy.

CLASSROOM/ASSEMBLY ACTIVITY

- Split the class in two and ask each group to imagine they have 'political power' for a day to pass new laws. What laws would they pass? Ask the two groups to debate the new laws from opposite viewpoints, saying why they should/should not be passed.

- Ask pupils to think of something that has made, or would make them very angry. Examples could include seeing someone kicking a dog or bullying a younger child, seeing loved ones being hurt or upset, or something in the wider world they think is wrong. How would they put the wrong thing right?

- Using examples from home or school, ask pupils to take turns to say, 'I think it is unfair when ...' (Examples from home could include an argument about watching TV, about restrictions on access to Internet, social media or to XBoxes.)

- Ask pupils if they know that they have rights too. Explain that these rights are mentioned in a special agreement, also written by the United Nations. It is called the *United Nations Convention on the Rights of the Child*. It gives a list of the things that governments must do to protect children and to ensure their rights are respected. The Convention says that each child has the right to go to school, to have health care and to be protected from harm and cruelty. It says that children must not become soldiers in an army. Study this online or download photocopies of the Convention in child-friendly form.[21]

1.6 Non-violent protest

Explain to the class that peaceful protest can be a powerful and useful way for citizens to show their concerns in a democracy. Many of our democratic laws have come about or been influenced in this way. Protesting about something means trying to change how other people think and how they behave. We want things to be done differently. The people whose behaviour we want to change are the people in charge of things, whether at home, at school or in the community. Most of the time, protesting is done in a peaceful way.

Explain that terrorists think that peaceful ways of protesting are useless or take too long. Other people think that using violence is *always wrong*, however unfair things are.

Terrorists think that violence is the only way to change things

Mahatma Gandhi

Introduce or remind pupils of the Indian independence leader Mohandas K (Mahatma) Gandhi (1869–1948). Ask the class if they know who he is and why he was famous. Explain that India was ruled by Britain for about one hundred years. It was part of the British Empire. Mahatma Gandhi was very unhappy about this. He wanted Indians to rule themselves, to be independent. Gandhi thought it was very unfair that the British ruled India, not Indians, but he decided that violence was not the way to win independence. He believed in *ahimsa*, a Sanskrit word which means avoiding the use of violence against any living creature.

Gandhi once said,

There are many **causes** *that I am prepared to die for, but no causes that I am prepared to kill for.*

Explain that Mahatma Gandhi had a different idea about how to protest against British rule in India. He called it *satyagraha*, which literally means 'truth force'. He thought that Indians should protest with the truth, and that this truth was stronger than violence. Gandhi wanted Indians to disobey the British laws that were unfair to Indians, and to do so in great numbers. He called for 'civil disobedience'.

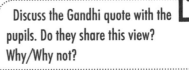

Discuss the Gandhi quote with the pupils. Do they share this view? Why/Why not?

Illustrate an example of Gandhi's campaign of civil disobedience with the following example:

There was a law in India that said a tax had to be paid to the British government on every packet of salt that was sold. Indians were not allowed to collect or sell it themselves. Gandhi thought this was very unfair because salt is a natural product and one which people need and use every day. To protest about this, on 12 March 1930, he and 78 followers set off to march 241 miles to the sea at Dandi, in the state of Gujarat. Along the way he spoke to crowds of people and thousands joined the march. When they arrived three weeks later at the seashore, Gandhi picked up a piece of salt from the sand where the water had evaporated. Just by this action he had broken the law. After this, millions of other Indians joined the protest in different ways. Over 80,000 people, including Gandhi himself, were put in prison for the salt *satyagraha* campaign. During his lifetime Gandhi spent many years in prison for his campaigns of civil disobedience.

Ask pupils to think of examples of being disobedient at home and at school. Why is this different from civil disobedience?

Explain that civil disobedience can take different forms. Nowadays it often refers to sit-ins, that is, when people sit down in, or occupy, a building or public space. Sometimes people sit or lie down on roads or railways, blocking them with their bodies so that traffic cannot pass.

Dr Martin Luther King Jr

Explain that Mahatma Gandhi's ideas about violence and on civil disobedience had an important impact on a man who lived thousands of miles from India. Introduce or remind pupils about Dr Martin Luther King Jr (1929–1968) leader of the civil rights **movement** in the United States during the 1950s and 60s.

Remind the class that like India, America was once part of the British Empire. But unlike India, America went to war against Britain in order to become free from British rule. In 1776, while the war was still being fought, thirteen American colonies declared themselves to be independent. The US Declaration of Independence says that everyone is created equal, and that each person has certain rights that cannot be taken away. These rights include life, liberty and the search for happiness.

Explain that almost two hundred years later, until the late 1960s, many black Americans – almost all of them descended from slaves who had been captured in Africa and sold to white plantation owners – were denied the same rights in law as white Americans, and suffered from *racial discrimination*. This was much worse in the southern states of America where African Americans were treated as second-class citizens and most could not vote.

The people who were angry and protested about this formed what is called the civil rights movement. A movement is a group of people or organisations that share the same goals. One of the heroines of the civil rights movement was a black woman called Rosa Parks. In December 1955 she was arrested in Montgomery, Alabama, when she refused to give up her seat on a bus to a white passenger. After this the civil rights protest movement spread wider and wider. The civil rights movement demanded **equal rights** for African Americans in all areas, including education, health care, housing and the right to vote. An organisation of white Americans called the Klu Klux Klan aimed to resist all these improvements and to terrorise the black population. Its members carried out many violent attacks against black Americans and leaders of the civil rights movement and firebombed their homes. Martin Luther King believed in non-violence, like Mahatma Gandhi. His word for *satyagraha* was 'soul force', the force of the soul.

CLASSROOM/ASSEMBLY ACTIVITY

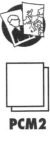

Distribute copies of PCM2 and explain that, in August 1963, Martin Luther King led a protest march of 250,000 people to Washington, where he made a famous speech. It is called the 'I have a dream' speech. Read the following extract from the speech and discuss it with the class:

PCM2

> *Let us not seek to satisfy our thirst for freedom by drinking from the cup of bitterness and hatred. We must forever conduct our struggle on the high plane of dignity and discipline. We must not allow our creative protest to* **degenerate** *into physical violence. Again and again, we must rise to the majestic heights of meeting physical force with soul force …*
>
> *I have a dream that one day on the red hills of Georgia, the sons of former slaves and the sons of former slave owners will be able to sit down together at the table of brotherhood … I have a dream that my four little children will one day live in a nation where they will not be judged by the color of their skin but by the content of their character.*

He repeated the words, 'I have a dream', several times to imagine a future where all Americans would live peacefully together and enjoy the same freedoms. In his speech he asked black Americans not to use violence to win their goals, even though much violence had been used against them.

In 1968 Martin Luther King was murdered on the balcony of the hotel where he was staying in Memphis, Tennessee. A few months later most of the laws that discriminated against African Americans had been **abolished**.

Read and discuss with pupils Paul Cookson's 2001 poem:

Let no one steal your dreams

Let no one steal your dreams
Let no one tear apart
The burning of **ambition**
That fires the drive inside your heart
Let no one steal your dreams
Let no one tell you that you can't
Let no one hold you back
Let no one tell you that you won't
Set your sights and keep them fixed
Set your sights on high
Let no one steal your dreams
Your only limit is the sky
Let no one steal your dreams
Follow your heart
Follow your soul
For only when you follow them
Will you feel truly whole
Set your sights and keep them fixed
Set your sights on high
Let no one steal your dreams
Your only limit is the sky

Anti-war protests

Explain that sometimes, when the government of a country takes a decision, not all of the population will agree with it. Citizens protest if they think the government is going to introduce a law that is unfair. Sometimes people protest about a government's foreign policy. In 2003 many people around the world did not support the invasion of Iraq by the United States, Britain and Australia. (The governments of those countries thought that Iraq's president, Saddam Hussein, had powerful weapons that he might use against them.) On 15 February 2003, protest marches took place in around 600 cities across the world, involving between six and ten million people. There were protests in the US and in almost every European country, as well as in Canada, Australia, India, South Africa and New Zealand. About three quarters of a million people marched in Australia's state capitals. There were protests in 70 Canadian towns and cities of which the largest was in Montreal, where around 150,000 people marched, despite the freezing temperature of -30°C.

Emphasise that in almost every city where demonstrations took place the protest was peaceful, and very few arrests were made. The protests did not stop the invasion, which went ahead (although Canada did not join the invasion force, perhaps because of **public opinion** against the war).

Stress that the people who went on the protest marches were angry about the reasons for going to war with Iraq. They wanted their voices to be heard, even if their governments didn't listen. But none of them thought that the right way to protest was through violence.

CLASSROOM/ASSEMBLY ACTIVITY

■ Ask pupils to think of dreams that they have for a better future. Invite them to make posters to illustrate the dream.

■ Encourage the class to think of things they might want to protest about. Ask them to work out how they could organise the protest in a peaceful way.

1.7 Changing things through violence

Remind pupils of the little brother/sister who damages the older child's book/game/toy. Ask them to repeat what the correct course of action was. Suggest that if the older child went to an adult and showed what the little brother/sister had done, most adults would be sympathetic. They would promise to make things OK, and might even buy a new book/game/toy. But if the older child had punched and kicked the little brother/sister the adults would not be sympathetic. They certainly wouldn't buy a new book/game/toy. What would they say? They'd say using violence was wrong and that it was an unacceptable behaviour.

Give pupils another example of how violence can harm peaceful protest.

STORYLINE

Feel free to change names, place names and circumstances as appropriate. Storylines could vary as follows:

The Riverside Park protest: there are plans to build over a pleasant, green part of town with a shopping centre or similar. A (non-violent) protest group is set up, and seems to have much support. But a few of its members are impatient. They kidnap the baby daughter of the builder whose company has the contract to build the shopping centre. They say they will free the baby if the builder promises not to build. The kidnappers are caught and the baby is safe, but the protest group loses all support, and the shopping centre is built after all.

The Forest protest: there are plans to cut down the trees in a large area of forest to make way for an industrial or agricultural project. The forest provides a traditional livelihood for many villages in the area, which have few alternative sources of income. A non-violent protest group is set up, but a few of its members are impatient and take violent action …

The Pipeline protest: in an area traditionally given over to fishing and farming, a foreign oil company intends to pump oil from below the seabed through a series of pipelines. A non-violent protest group is set up, but a few of its members are impatient and take violent action …

The Riverside Park protest

Introduce Joe Smith. Joe is angry about plans for a new shopping centre in the Riverside area of his town, Bowmarket. If it goes ahead, the shopping centre will be built in an area where now there is a park. People go to Riverside Park to play football, to jog, to walk their dogs and have picnics. Joe doesn't mind about not being able to walk a dog, he doesn't have one. In fact he has two cats, called Smudge and Billy. Joe doesn't play football either; at weekends he goes fishing. But he likes to walk through the park sometimes. Most of all he thinks it's important for everyone to be able to use the park and enjoy its open spaces. Joe wants the park to stay a park, not just for himself, but for all the people of Bowmarket. He feels so strongly about this that he sets up a group to protest about the building plans. He calls it the 'Save Riverside Group'. He talks to lots of people he knows and persuades them to join.

The members of the Save Riverside Group are *angry*, and feel that what is happening is *unfair and wrong*. They want as many people as possible to know about their protest and join the group, even people they don't know. They want to *send a message* to the people who are in charge of things – the mayor and town council of Bowmarket.

The Save Riverside Group needs to do something that will attract everyone's attention. One Saturday morning, Joe's protest group organises a protest march through Riverside Park and into the town centre of Bowmarket. About 500 people go on the march waving banners that say 'Keep Riverside Green!' and 'Hands off Riverside Park!' The local TV station comes out to film them. Reporters come from the local paper. Lots of people who didn't know about the plans to build a shopping centre come out of houses and shops to see what's going on, and to listen to what the protesters have to say. This is exactly what Joe wants. People are paying attention to the protest. They are getting publicity.   >>

The march ends up outside the Town Hall, where Joe hands in a letter for the mayor. This letter is called a **petition**. It asks the mayor and the town council to change their minds and refuse permission for the shopping centre. It explains why Riverside Park should be saved. It asks for the shopping centre, if it is needed, to be built somewhere else. The petition has been signed by 900 people. Joe believes that the Save Riverside Group can change the way people think. This is the same as saying its members can *change public opinion*. Public opinion may then persuade the mayor and the town council that the plan is a bad idea. The protesters want to change the way things are done in their community. What they want is called *political power.* Political power is the power to decide how things are done.

What Joe doesn't know is that not everyone in the Save Riverside Group agrees with the way he is running the protest group. John, Amy and Ben are plotting behind his back. They think that peaceful protest takes too long and isn't getting results. They want to do something very daring, something that will really make people sit up and take notice. They want more publicity for the Save Riverside Group. On the same Saturday morning they start out on the march with everyone else. Then, half way to the town centre they slip away and head down a quiet side street. John keeps watch as Ben and Amy climb a wall and drop down into the back garden of a house. The house belongs to Mr Elliot Brown, the owner of a company called Bowmarket Builders. Bowmarket Builders is the company that will build the shopping centre if it goes ahead. Under a big tree there is a pram with a baby sleeping in it. The baby in the pram is Mr Brown's daughter, Rachel.

Amy wraps Rachel in a blanket and takes her out of the pram. She passes the baby up to Ben and he passes her down to John who puts her into a sports bag. The two climb back over the wall and they all take Rachel away to a hiding place. John phones the Browns' house and puts on a false voice so he won't be recognised. He says they don't want to hurt Rachel, and as soon as they have a promise that the shopping centre won't be built over Riverside Park, they will bring her back.

Joe knows nothing about the kidnap. If he had known, he would have been very angry, he would have prevented it. By Saturday evening, everyone in Bowmarket knows about Rachel. People are shocked that a baby has been kidnapped. On Sunday afternoon, police get a tip-off. They go to Amy's house and find Rachel in the attic. The attic is very cold, and Rachel is coughing. She is also hungry. She might have become very ill, she could even have died. Amy, John and Ben are arrested. The police want to arrest Joe too, but he convinces them that he had nothing to do with the kidnap.

After this everyone was furious with the Save Riverside Group. They said that kidnapping an innocent baby was a terrible thing to do, even if they hadn't meant to hurt her. Public opinion turned against the whole group, not just the three who had taken the baby. The Save Riverside Group broke up. A few months later, Bowmarket Builders started work on Riverside Retail Park.

Ask pupils what they think about the Save Riverside Group. What would they have done if they had been members? Does anyone have any sympathy with what Amy, John and Ben did?

Joe was sad about the way things turned out, but he understood the reason. He still thought that the goal of the protest movement was right, that Riverside Park should be kept green. But because some members of his protest group had kidnapped a little baby who could have died, everyone stopped supporting them.

What went wrong? Explain that even though the *goal* may have been a good one, the *methods* were *wrong*. Kidnapping a baby and putting her life in danger was going too far. In this case, if the protest group had only used peaceful methods of protest, they might well have won, and the shopping centre would not have been built.

Explain that Ben, Amy and John are not people we would really think of as terrorists. They didn't want to hurt Rachel Brown or frighten her. They wanted to terrorise her father for a few hours and to make him agree to what they asked. Even so, what they did was a kind of terrorism. They *kidnapped* a little baby. They held her *hostage*. They had a *message*, not for their victim, the baby, but for her father. None of them actually knew Mr Elliot Brown personally but he was their *enemy*. They wanted him to promise *not to do something* – not to build the shopping centre. Rachel's parents were certainly *terrorised*, because they had no idea where their baby was. And because Rachel Brown had been kidnapped, all the other parents of babies were terrorised too. Ben, Amy and John got carried away with their foolish ideas, and they paid the price: they were put on trial and went to prison.

Explain that terrorists are rather different from Ben, Amy and John. They may start with the same feelings that we – and the Save Riverside Group – know about, like anger, disappointment and a sense that things are unfair. But terrorists' anger goes much, much deeper. They feel so strongly that things are unfair that they are willing to kill and be killed in their attempt to change things.

Terrorism is not just protesting in a violent way. Terrorism is a kind of war, usually started by a weaker group against a stronger one. In this book most of our study of terrorism is about individuals or groups whom we describe as *non-state*. We call them this because their actions are not carried out in the name of a country or state. They use violence because they feel they are the victims of unfairness, and they want to take revenge against an enemy whom they blame for the unfairness.

SUMMARY UNIT 1

■ Discuss with the class what they most remember about the Unit.

■ Bring pupils back to the idea of terrorism as a kind of cooking pot in which different ingredients are found. If certain ingredients are not in the pot then what we're looking at probably isn't terrorism. It's a bit like saying that unless there are (at least) meat, onions and potatoes in a dish then we can't call it Irish Stew.

■ Draw a picture of a large cooking pot on a sheet of paper and pin it to the classroom wall. Pupils can write labels to stick or pin on the pot. Each label represents a different ingredient.

We have learned that the following ingredients must be present if we are to call something terrorism:

● the *use or threat of violence to cause terror*, usually by individuals or groups not acting for a country or state (*non-state individuals*)

● *grievances* (strong feelings of anger, disappointment and hatred) that are blamed on an enemy, and the desire to take revenge

● the use of violence *against 'ordinary people'* or *civilians*

● *goals of political power* that are not just for one person but for a community

● the aim of attracting as much attention, or *publicity*, as possible

● the aim of *sending a message* to change the behaviour of an authority or the people in charge

● the belief that *violence is the only way* to reach the goals

■ Remind the class about unfairness, discrimination and rights. Unfairness and discrimination make people angry because it means they do not have the same rights as everyone else. They have grievances that make them unhappy. There are lots of ways of protesting about this. Some methods are not violent, and other methods are violent. Violence may do harm to peaceful protest.

CLASSROOM/ASSEMBLY ACTIVITY

■ Show the class the child-friendly wording of the Convention on the Rights of the Child (see endnote 21). It says children should be brought up in the spirit of *'peace, dignity, tolerance, freedom, equality and solidarity.'* Ask them to discuss the significance of each of the words, and why they are important.

■ Ask (older) pupils to think of words that mean the *opposite* of those above, for example the opposites:

peace ↔ war or conflict
dignity ↔ indignity, humiliation or disrespect
tolerance ↔ intolerance
freedom ↔ slavery, imprisonment
equality ↔ inequality
solidarity ↔ discord, disunity, disagreement

■ Mahatma Gandhi and Martin Luther King were very unhappy that Indians and African Americans respectively were not treated with *dignity*. Ask pupils to explore the theme of dignity in home or school life and how this can be expressed.

■ Help the class to research a real or imaginary issue of local relevance that is controversial, eg plans to build a road bypass; chop down trees in a forest; build a leisure park. The class splits into two or more groups. The groups study and then present the issue from different angles. The group in favour should give reasons why the proposal is a good one; the opposing group should present its arguments against and a plan for organising the protest. The issue is presented to assembly and a debate can be held. For younger age groups the activity could be focused on a school or home activity eg a question of whether or not to adopt a pet from a shelter, build a fishpond, garage or tool shed, or change a room in the house.

Unit 2:
'Terrorism' and History

KEY VOCABULARY

assassin: someone who deliberately seeks out and kills a particular individual

sacrifice: a gift or offering of great value, usually as part of religious worship

suffrage: the right to vote

general election: a vote to choose the people who will govern a country

just cause: a set of reasons which are good or noble

motto: a saying or slogan that contains a message

martyr: term used to describe someone who dies or is put to death because of a belief, principle or cause

hunger strike: a refusal to eat until a request or demand is met

patriotic: loyal, showing love for one's country

universal suffrage: the right to vote for all adults (usually persons over the age of 18)

ban: to make something unlawful

massacre: the violent killing of a large number of people

sabotage: to deliberately damage something so that it does not work properly

domination: power over other people

cherish: to hold dearly, to treasure

ideal: (noun) the best outcome for the individual or group concerned

harmony: peace, agreement, order (also a musical term)

negotiate: to make a bargain, find an agreement

suppression: the putting down or holding back of something/someone

definition: a way of describing exactly what something *is*

universal definition: a way of describing something that all countries can agree on

Aim and content of Unit 2

In this Unit, pupils look at different kinds of violent behaviour over the centuries that could be (or were) called terrorism. In each of the examples given, *reasons* and *goals* differed widely but all derived from a belief in a *just cause* and a conviction that the only *method* of reaching their goal was the use of violence. Unit 2 demonstrates, first, that something called 'terrorism' – undefined – has existed for centuries and is not carried out by members of any one country, race, region or faith. Many forms of political violence have nothing at all to do with religion, as was the case with the Suffragettes. Second, it illustrates the difficulty of reaching a definition of terrorism when the context in which violence takes place varies so widely and when opportunities for peaceful protest may be limited. Groups or individuals who may be considered terrorists by some people may be called heroes or martyrs by others. The concept of martyrdom is introduced for older pupils and its controversial place in terrorist violence is discussed. Finally the Unit shows that judgements on whether or not violence is justified tend to be highly subjective and may change with the passing of time; it also looks at the difficulties of finding a common agreement on what to call terrorism.

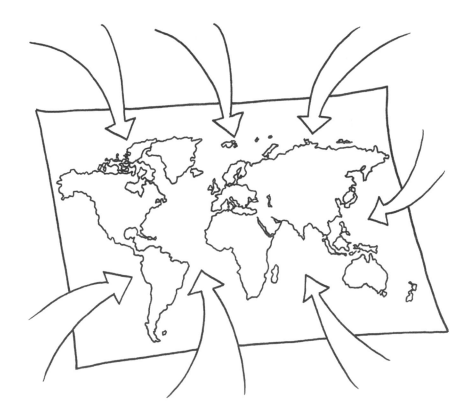

Terrorism can occur anywhere in the world

LEARNING OUTCOMES

By the end of Unit 2, pupils will be able to:

■ ascertain that the use of violence for political or religious goals is not new but has been practised for centuries, and that it does not derive from any particular country, religion or part of the world

■ understand how violence is used to attract attention and to cause fear and that it is possible to agree with the *reasons* and *goals* of a group but disagree with what it does (its *methods*)

■ see the use of violence in the context of a *just cause*, and begin to understand why it is so difficult to define terrorism

■ represent and debate opposing sides of a political argument (the Suffragettes' use of violence)

■ describe the Nobel Peace Prize and the criteria for winning it, with reference to Nelson Mandela and Malala Yousafzai

Older pupils will be able to:

■ understand the concepts of martyrs and martyrdom. This is first introduced in a non-religious context before the (more sensitive) issue of religious martyrdom in a terrorist context is discussed

RECOMMENDED MATERIALS

Map of the world

Large sheets of white paper on which to display quotes and comments

Paper and drawing materials

Photo images of:
• the Suffragettes
• Nelson Mandela (x2)

Picture images of:
• religious symbols (crucifix, kippah...) and places of worship (church, gurdwara, synagogue, mosque)

Computers on which to research: background to Suffragettes or downloads of information on their activities; background to *Nobel Peace Prize* or appropriate Internet downloads

Notes for teachers

The Unit does not try to define terrorism, and this discussion should be postponed, although pupils should be encouraged to explore the issues of violence and just cause. The issue of martyrdom is particularly sensitive. Resist attempts to elicit approval or disapproval of acts of martyrdom in whatever form. It is enough to say that those who died for their beliefs are often called martyrs by those who share those beliefs. Many others will not share the beliefs and will reject the term.

2.1 Introduction

Begin by asking pupils whether they think terrorism is new or old. Explain that it is very old indeed. Suggest that if we want to understand what terrorism is, it can be useful to go back in time to look at different ways in which violence has been used to achieve political or religious goals. Point out that some of the people and groups that will be discussed in this Unit are very different to the people we might think of as terrorists today. We might not call them terrorists at all. All the same, they have something in common with what we know about terrorism: they felt violence was necessary and it was the only way to achieve their goals.

Let's look back in history

2.2 Assassins, Thugs and Suffragettes

In this Unit, use a map of the world to show pupils the different countries where the following examples of political violence occurred.

It will become evident as work progresses that no one area or country is 'responsible' for terrorism.

Assassins

Ask pupils if they have heard the word **assassin** and if they know what it means. If not, explain that an assassin is someone who kills or *assassinates* another person. In fact the name comes from a religious group (of *Nizari Ismailis*) called the Assassins who lived almost a thousand years ago in Persia (now called Iran) and Syria.

Explain that the Assassins were afraid that their way of life was under threat from a larger, more powerful religious group that ruled Persia. The Assassins wanted to get rid of the ruling group and run Persia in their own way. They felt it was their *duty* to kill in order to protect their way of life. Young men were trained to be skilled fighters, and then were sent out on their mission. They often carried out the murders in a public place and on a public holiday. The idea was that as many people as possible would be watching. They always used a dagger although more deadly weapons were available, and only attacked the most important and powerful individuals. Unlike terrorists today, they never harmed ordinary people going about their business. An Assassin knew he would be arrested and almost certainly put to death afterwards but did not try to escape. To survive would have been a disgrace.[22]

Thugs

As a warm-up activity, start a round of simple word association: eg think of a word like 'sea' and ask pupils what words they associate with it (eg fish, boats, swimming). Repeat this once or twice with other words. Then do this same procedure for the word *thug*. We call someone a thug if their behaviour is nasty or rough. (Link this to ideas about bullying.)

Explain that thug comes from a Hindi word *thag*, meaning thief, or someone who deceives another. The Thugs were members of a branch of Hinduism who lived in northern India for centuries until about two hundred years ago. Like all Hindus, they worshipped the goddess Kali. But the Thugs were different because they felt they had a duty to kill human beings as a **sacrifice** to please her. On certain holy days they left their homes and jobs and lay in wait for travellers along the roadside. The Thugs pretended to befriend them and travelled some distance with them. Then they strangled the travellers with a silk tie without spilling any blood. The goal in this case was not to win political power but to win the favour of the goddess. They certainly terrorised large numbers of travellers. Hindus still worship the goddess Kali today but they do not believe in human sacrifice, and there are no more Thugs in India.

Suffragettes

Introduce the Suffragette movement, and explain that the name comes from the word **suffrage**, meaning the right to vote. Remind pupils that at the beginning of the 20th century two thirds of British men could vote and stand as members of parliament, while women could only stand and vote in local elections. Since the 1860s there had been some support for women's suffrage among both men and women, but the movement did not have strong leadership. In 1903 an organisation called The Women's Social and Political Union (WSPU) was formed by a Mrs Emmeline Pankhurst with her daughters, Christabel and Sylvia, in the city of Manchester. The Suffragettes, as they were called, wanted women to have equal rights with men, in particular the right to vote. There was a **general election** in 1906. Some of the candidates to parliament promised before the election that they would help women to win the right to vote if they were elected. They did not succeed. A short debate was held in the House of Commons, but most members of parliament (MPs) were against the idea. One stood up and said that only women with 'masculine minds' could be interested in politics. Another said that women should not get the vote because they were 'nervous and emotional'.

Ask pupils to imagine how the Suffragettes must have felt when they heard those remarks. Suggest that the Suffragettes were *angry* and *disappointed*.

Display the quote, 'Women should not have the vote because they are nervous and emotional' on a large sheet of paper or on a whiteboard. Ask the girls how they would feel it they were told they couldn't do a favourite activity because they were 'nervous and emotional'. Ask the class to think of an equivalent saying about boys/men, that they couldn't do something because they were too … ? Why would this also be unfair?

Remind pupils about the ideas discussed in Unit 1 of civil rights and fair/unfairness.

Suffragettes did not have the right to speak in Parliament because they were women. But they wanted to *send a message* to MPs that they were angry. They wanted to explain their *reasons* for being angry and to win support for their cause. To do this the Suffragettes needed publicity, but newspaper editors often refused to publish articles supporting them. So they looked for new ways of attracting attention. They chained themselves to the railings of Buckingham Palace and of 10 Downing Street, official home of the British prime minister. They interrupted speakers during political meetings by shouting for the right to vote and were often kicked and beaten by police who pulled them away. They began by protesting in a peaceful way, but they discovered that people noticed them more when they carried out violent actions.

Pause the lesson at this point and ask the class how they feel about the Suffragettes: do they feel sympathetic towards them, angry (on their behalf), or were they going a bit too far?

They smashed the windows of important buildings and big department stores, poured acid and tar and dropped lighted torches into letter-boxes and cut telephone wires. They set fire to cricket pavilions, golf clubhouses where only men could be members, racecourse stands and churches. They attacked churches because the church authorities did not approve of women having the vote. They damaged paintings and statues in art galleries. They threatened members of parliament with violence and firebombed their homes. Death threats were made against the King, George V, in speeches and letters. Mrs Pankhurst said that 'all the methods of war' were allowed in the battle for the vote, although she also said human (and animal) life should not be harmed.[23] The newspapers talked of 'mad women', and 'dangerous and wicked violence' carried out by 'terrorists'. Hundreds of women were arrested.

Explain that many people stopped supporting the Suffragettes because of their violent actions. They thought that the Suffragettes had a **just cause** – that is, that their goal was a good and noble one, and they had good reasons for being angry. But they couldn't support the Suffragettes because they felt their violent methods were wrong.

Ask pupils if they have heard of the famous horse race called the Derby. It takes place in the English town of Epsom every year. At the Derby in 1913 a Suffragette called Emily Davison ran out in front of the racehorse Amner, owned by King George V, tried to grab its bridle and was knocked to the ground. She died a few days later. (Neither horse nor jockey were badly hurt.) Thousands of Suffragettes turned out for her funeral and the Suffragette **motto**, 'Deeds not Words!' was carved on Emily's gravestone.

> **OPTIONAL INFORMATION FOR OLDER PUPILS**
>
> **Martyrs**
>
> By her action, Emily Davison became a **martyr** in the eyes of the Suffragettes. Ask pupils if they know what a martyr is. Explain that it is a term that describes someone who is killed or chooses to die because of a belief or cause. The willingness to die is a sign of how important the beliefs are to that person. All through history there are examples of religious martyrs who have been killed by people of a different faith because they would not give up or change their beliefs. Those who died thought that their god or their religion expected them to make this sacrifice. They died willingly because they believed the cause was a noble one and that they would be rewarded or blessed by the god they had suffered for.
>
> Explain that Emily Davison's protest had nothing to do with religion, and she probably did not want to die. (She had a return train   >>

ticket to London in her pocket.) It's thought that she may have been trying to attach a WSPU banner to the horse's bridle and fell under its hooves by mistake. But she must have realised she was risking her life by her action. She had once written that to give up one's life for liberty was 'glorious, selfless, inspiring.'

When we study terrorism we find the word 'martyr' is sometimes used with an extra meaning. Explain that some people – called martyrs by their supporters – kill other people at the same time as they kill themselves. If they use explosives to blow themselves and others up they are called *suicide bombers*. In Sri Lanka, young women, some only in their teens, were used as suicide bombers. They were members of an organisation called the Liberation Tigers of Tamil Eelam, or Tamil Tigers. Because they were girls, the security guards who were protecting people and buildings were less likely to stop and search them. The Tamil Tigers were not fighting for a religious cause but in order to win a homeland for the Tamil population of Sri Lanka in the northeast of the island.

> **TIP**
>
> Although suicide bombers are called martyrs by their supporters, many people would think of them as murderers. Allow pupils some time to discuss their ideas about sacrifice and martyrs.

Explain that by the summer of 1914, over a thousand Suffragettes had been sent to prison for periods of weeks or months, and women still did not have the right to vote. When they went to prison, most Suffragettes went on **hunger strike**. That means they refused to eat. They did this to protest about their poor treatment in prison and to attract more attention to themselves. The government didn't want any of them to die so most of the women were force-fed: tubes were put into their throats or noses to make sure they took some food. It was extremely painful and unpleasant for them, and involved violent treatment by the prison guards. As more violence was used against them, the Suffragettes' own use of violence increased.

Remind pupils that World War 1 started in August 1914. The British government decided to allow all the Suffragette prisoners to go free. Mrs Pankhurst and most Suffragettes decided to support the British government and the fighting forces. They decided that being **patriotic** – being loyal to their country and helping it – was the most important duty for a British citizen. It was even more important than the right to vote.

Explain that during World War 1 over five million British servicemen were abroad fighting for their country.[24] But the jobs they had left behind were important and had to be filled: a new workforce of women came forward. They took over many of the jobs that men had done in factories, on farms, and in shipyards. Women worked as bus conductors for the first time. Many women had never worked outside the home at all, but now they were doing heavy jobs like loading coal into train engines, rolling beer barrels at breweries and building ships.

Women in the United States also fought a long battle for the vote, starting in the mid 19th century. From 1890 individual states in the Union began to give women the right to vote, and from 1920, by law all American women over the age of 21 could vote. However state laws made it impossible for most black women to vote until after the civil rights movement of the 1960s and the murder of Martin Luther King forced a change (see Unit 1).

Remind the class what they have learned from the example of the Suffragettes. It shows:
(a) that violence makes people sit up and pay attention
(b) that people may stop supporting a cause when they decide that certain *methods* - being practised in their name - are wrong
(c) that it is possible to agree with the reasons and the *goals* of a group - in this case the vote for women - but disagree with its *methods*
(d) why people are thought of as martyrs: people who choose to die or suffer greatly for a cause they believe in. The cause is often, but not always, a religious one

Women also volunteered to work as nurses and doctors in military hospitals abroad.

Tell pupils that, in February 1918, before the war was over, the British parliament passed a new law. It gave the vote to women over 30 years of age who owned property or paid rent of at least £5 per year, or whose husbands did, or who had a university degree. It was not until ten years later, in 1928, that all women (and men) aged 21 or over had the right to vote. When all adults have the right to vote we call it **universal suffrage**.

Ask pupils to reflect on the Suffragettes and on what they did.

Emphasise the importance of their *methods* of protest: damaging buildings, threatening MPs and the King with violence, chaining themselves to railings, destroying letters, etc. Ask pupils what they think about these actions. Also remind pupils of the violence done to the women. They were often pushed around and kicked by police at political meetings, and were force-fed and treated with cruelty in prison.

Ask pupils why they think women were given the vote in 1918. Some people think the only reason was because they had worked so hard during the war. In other words, the vote was their *reward* for being patriotic, not for protesting. They think that the violent actions of the Suffragettes upset people and made politicians less keen to give them the vote, not more. Other people think the Suffragettes helped women in their fight for the vote.[25]

CLASSROOM/ASSEMBLY ACTIVITY

■ Use the words 'assassin' and 'thug' to reflect with the class on how words have come into English from other languages. British rule in India lasted for over one hundred years, so it is not surprising that many words were adopted into English in this period from Indian languages. Other examples include pyjamas, shampoo, jodhpurs and bungalow. Bungalow comes from the Hindi word *bangla* – meaning 'house in the Bengal style'. Ask pupils, where appropriate, for other examples of words from other countries or cultures into English from French or Italian (eg restaurant, pizzeria, rendezvous…); or Spanish (eg paella, cigar, vanilla, banana and armada).

■ Help pupils to devise a role-play involving a meeting between, on the one hand, the Suffragettes who used violent methods, and on the other, people who had supported them but no longer could because of the violence. Alternatively, this >>

could take the form of an exchange of letters. (Computers, if available, could be used for this activity.)

■ Ask pupils to imagine that Emily Davison had survived. Invite them to prepare questions to interview her. One pupil could take the role of Emily; another could be a witness to her action at the racecourse, another the interviewer.

■ With class assistance, put together a timeline for the Suffragettes' activities. (Again computers may be useful here.)

2.3 World War 2 and the French Resistance movement

Invite pupils to say what they know about World War 2, and about what life was like in their town or area during that time.

Explain that during the war Germany was ruled by Chancellor Adolf Hitler and the National-Socialist or Nazi party. In 1940 Germany invaded France and its army occupied a large part of France for four years. Nazi laws were very strict, and French people were not allowed to protest. If they did they could be killed. Thousands of French people joined a movement called the Resistance which worked secretly against the Germans. Its members used explosives to blow up railway lines and buildings used by the Germans, such as warehouses where fuel and weapons were stored. They deliberately killed people – usually German soldiers – but sometimes French people who were helping the Germans.

Suggest that some people might call the members of French Resistance 'terrorists' because of their violent methods. The Nazis certainly called them terrorists. In fact, almost everyone nowadays thinks of them as heroes. This is because they risked their lives to help France become a free country again and many had been tortured and/or killed. After the war thousands of Resistance members were awarded medals for bravery.

2.4 Nelson Mandela

Show the class a photo of Nelson Mandela and ask them if they know who he was and establish what they know about him.

And/or: Show the class two copies of the same photo, one with the word 'Terrorist!' written on it, the other with the words 'Hero, Man of Peace!' Invite the class to say which photo they think is more accurate and why. Ask them what they know about Nelson Mandela's life.

Provide background details as follows:

Nelson Mandela was one of the leaders of a political party called the African National Congress, or ANC. The ANC members were angry because the laws in South Africa were very unfair to black and coloured people. The political system in South Africa was called *apartheid*, which means 'apartness'. It *discriminated* between the different races in South Africa. People were divided into four groups: Whites, Blacks, Coloureds and Indians. Only Whites – those who had come to live in South Africa from European countries – could own land and vote. Black people, who were the native population of South Africa, had to live in what were called 'homelands'. These were often areas without clean water, electricity or decent houses. They had to ask permission to visit the white areas and were obliged to carry a special 'pass' that said who they were and where they could go. They had to go on separate buses, and couldn't sit in the same cinemas as white people. Schools, colleges and hospitals were all separate too.

Anyone who tried to protest about apartheid, even peacefully, ran the risk of being beaten, arrested or killed. In 1960 there were protests in a town called Sharpeville. 69 black people were killed – many had been shot in the back. That means they were probably running away. They had come out to protest peacefully and were not carrying arms.

Explain that the African National Congress was **banned** after this – in other words, it was not allowed to exist and it was a crime to be a member of it. But it kept going in secret. Many members had to go and live outside South Africa. After the 'Sharpeville **massacre**', as it was called, Nelson Mandela, together with other leading members of the ANC, decided that it was necessary to use violence – what they called 'armed struggle' – to fight apartheid in South Africa. Non-violent protest had failed: it had not stopped violence against South Africans, nor had it changed the behaviour of the country's rulers.

A new organisation was formed inside the ANC. It was called *Umkhonto we Sizwe*, or 'Spear of the Nation'. Its purpose was to carry out violent acts. But Nelson Mandela and his companions didn't begin by killing people, they began with a different sort of violence, called **sabotage**. Sabotage means deliberately damaging property and machinery so that they don't work. As we have seen, the members of the French Resistance did that too. The aim of sabotage is to make life as difficult as possible for the people who run the country.

Nelson Mandela did not hate white people, he wanted everyone to live together and have the same rights. He wanted equal rights and universal suffrage. Until that time the ANC had only used peaceful methods, and it was a very big and important decision to change to violent methods.

Nelson Mandela was arrested and sent to prison in 1962. In 1964 he was put on trial for being a terrorist leader and for planning to overthrow the government (although he was not accused of killing anyone). He was found guilty and sentenced to life imprisonment.

Discuss the Nelson Mandela trial quote with the class.

Explain that in 1973 over one hundred countries of the United Nations agreed that apartheid was a 'crime against humanity', that is, against all the human beings in the world. They said that Nelson Mandela's trial was unfair. In countries around the world, people went on marches to protest about apartheid in South Africa. Governments protested too. Many countries refused to trade with South Africa and South African sports teams were not allowed to play in international events. The United Nations said no one should sell weapons to South Africa, because weapons were being used against black South Africans.

During the 27 years that Nelson Mandela was in prison, the violence grew worse and many people were killed. A kind of war was going on between government forces and those who were fighting apartheid, with bombings and assassinations carried out by both sides. The South African government was in difficulties at home and it was under pressure from countries abroad to end its policy of apartheid.

In 1985 President P.W. Botha, speaking in parliament, offered Nelson Mandela his freedom on condition that he rejected the use of violence as a method of political change. From prison Mandela refused, calling on the government to give up *its* violence and get rid of the apartheid laws.

Eventually, the politicians and other white people who had supported apartheid in South Africa began to realise that they couldn't keep it going much longer. In February 1990 President F.W. de Klerk set Nelson Mandela free – without any conditions.

In the months that followed the government abolished all the apartheid laws and restrictions. From then on Nelson Mandela encouraged all South Africans to take the path of peace and not to think about revenge. This was difficult as the violence had been terrible and had gone on for so long. In 1993 Nelson Mandela and President F.W. de Klerk were together awarded the most important prize in the world for peace, the Nobel Peace Prize.

The country's very first elections with universal suffrage – where adults of every race could vote – took place in 1994. The African National Congress won most votes, and formed the first government of the 'rainbow nation'. Nelson Mandela became the country's first black president. In 30 years Nelson Mandela had gone from being called 'leader of a terrorist group' to 'hero and peacemaker', the president of a multiracial democracy.

> At Nelson Mandela's trial he said:
> *I have fought against white* **domination** *and I have fought against black domination. I have* **cherished** *the* **ideal** *of a democratic and free society in which all persons live together in* **harmony** *and with equal opportunities. It is an ideal which I hope to live for and to achieve. But if need be, it is an ideal for which I am prepared to die.*[26]

> In a message read out in public by his daughter, Nelson Mandela said,
> *Only free men can* **negotiate** *… I cannot and will not give any undertaking at a time when I and you, the people are not free.*[27]

OPTIONAL INFORMATION FOR OLDER PUPILS

Explain that terrorism is often called 'the weapon of the weak' against a stronger power. Terrorists are called *non-state* individuals or groups because they do not act for a state or country, and consider government authorities as the enemy. Their aim is to win power and force the authorities to change their behaviour. It can happen however that governments use violence and terror against their own population, or against a population over whom they rule. In this case the goal is not to *win* power, but to *strengthen* the power that the government already has. This was the meaning of the word 'terrorism' when it first came into use during the so-called 'Reign of Terror' of the French Revolution in 1793–94. One could say that the Nazis in Germany used 'state' terrorism against part of their own population, especially Jews, as did South African governments during the apartheid period. Britain also used violence to strengthen the power and wealth of her Empire. In the nineteenth century Britain tried to make China accept imports of opium produced in India and make opium use legal. The aim was to balance all the payments Britain was making to China for tea. When China refused, Britain went to war twice and won.

TIP The Treasure box activity is to encourage pupils to consider/discuss what things they really value/treasure and to provoke an understanding of how they may feel if these 'treasures/values' were threatened.

CLASSROOM/ASSEMBLY ACTIVITY

■ Invite pupils to write down a list of things that they *cherish* or treasure. Encourage them to put items such as health, happiness, education, etc, into their treasure box rather than material goods.

■ Alternatively, ask them to imagine or draw three different boxes: one with things they could easily do without, one with things they would miss and one with things they need and treasure and that they couldn't live without.

■ Ask the class why South Africa is called the 'rainbow nation'. Are there other countries we can say this of?

■ Invite pupils to discuss the Nobel Peace Prize and what someone has to do to win it. Remind pupils of the award to the 2014 joint winners, Malala Yousafzai and Kailash Satyarthi 'for their struggle against the **suppression** of children and young people and for the right of all children to education.' Invite pupils to research their lives (online if computers available) and have a class discussion about their work.

2.5 What do they have in common and how are they different?

Discuss with pupils what, if anything, the Assassins, Thugs, Suffragettes, the French Resistance and the African National Congress have in common. Suggest that what they all have in common is that they used violence. All of them felt they had good reasons for using violence. They all believed they had a good or a *just cause.*

Now ask pupils what the differences are.

The Thugs are different in two ways: (1) because as far as we know they didn't want political power, they wanted a religious reward, and (2) they were not angry about discrimination or unfair laws.

The Assassins, the Suffragettes, the French Resistance and the ANC all had grievances – reasons for being angry about laws that treated them unfairly. They felt that peaceful protest was either not possible or had not worked, and that violence was necessary to achieve their goals.

The Suffragettes were different again. They threatened and used considerable violence and their actions could easily have resulted in the death of or severe injury to others. But they didn't kill anyone. The Suffragettes thought that violence was necessary, especially as violence was being used against them at protest meetings and in prison, but many other people disagreed. Peaceful protest *was* possible in Britain. People could say what they liked and no one was sent to prison for disagreeing with the government.

The situation was very different in France during World War 2. France was occupied by a foreign power and French people who resisted the occupation could be shot. In South Africa too the non-white population took great risks by protesting. It was a crime to belong to the African National Congress and even peaceful protesters could be killed. Where peaceful protest is not allowed some people feel that violence is the only weapon they have.

2.6 Terrorism – a universal agreement?

Suggest that, when we look at the examples from history in 2.2–2.4, we might think that none of them were terrorism. Or that some were terrorism, and others were not. We would almost certainly agree that many of the reasons were good. They had strong grievances and had a just cause. A *just cause* is a goal that we think is a good or noble one. Most people would say that the Suffragettes had a just cause because women have the same right to vote as men. We would agree that the French Resistance movement had a just cause because its members wanted France to be ruled by French people, not by Nazi

Ask the class to reflect on what Nelson Mandela said in a TV interview in 2000:

> *I was called a terrorist yesterday, but when I came out of jail many people embraced me, including my enemies, and that is what I normally tell other people, who say those who are struggling for liberation in their country are terrorists. I tell them that I was also a terrorist yesterday, but, today, I am admired by the very people who said I was one.*[28]

Germany. We would agree that Nelson Mandela and the African National Congress were right to be angry and protest about apartheid in South Africa because the government treated black and coloured people very badly.

Remind the class that public opinion today is very different to what it was 20, 100 or 200 years ago. People's views change over the years. There is hardly anyone now who would say that women should not be allowed to vote, or that only white people should rule South Africa, although many did at the time.

Explain that our study of groups who used violence in the past has brought us to an important new point. Remind the class that at the beginning of our study we said it was difficult to say what terrorism *is*. So we looked at what *isn't* terrorism. We learned why a cat chasing a mouse *isn't* terrorism, and why someone who bullies *isn't* a terrorist. The examples from history show us why it is still difficult to say what terrorism *is*.

Suggest that the examples in this Unit have taken us a bit further. We can understand why people are angry and why they have grievances. We may share their reasons for being angry and agree with their goals. But, even if things are very unfair and even if there is a just cause – is it right to use violence to change things? Can there ever be 'good' violence on the one side and 'bad' violence on the other – the one we call terrorism? If so, how do we decide?

Explain that these are very, very difficult questions. We may agree with Mahatma Gandhi that violence is always wrong, however good the cause. Or we may feel that violence may occasionally be right under certain circumstances. The problem is that what *you* feel is right may not seem right to your next door neighbour or to your teacher or to someone in another town or country. There is no agreed **definition**.

Suggest to pupils that what we really need is a way of saying what terrorism is that isn't just our own opinion. What we want is a **universal definition** of terrorism.

Ask pupils if they remember how the word universal is used. Universal suffrage means the vote for all adults. A universal definition of terrorism is an agreement on what terrorism *is* that every country can share, as we have with the United Nations Convention on the Rights of the Child. Governments and clever people have been trying to find a universal definition of terrorism for years. At least 150 different suggestions have been put forward but there is still no agreement. So it's hardly surprising if we find it difficult in the classroom. We will discuss this more in the following Units of the Handbook.

SUMMARY UNIT 2

■ The use of violence for a religious or political reward is not something recent, but has existed for centuries.

■ People who use this type of violence believe that it is necessary to do so. They believe they have a *just cause*.

■ People have very different views about whether, and in what circumstances, violence is just. The same people can be called terrorists by some and heroes by others.

■ People's views change with time.

CLASSROOM/ASSEMBLY ACTIVITY

■ Religion is sometimes linked to terrorism but the main religions have many things in common. Show pupils pictures of different religious symbols and key words which are common to all faiths and some which are specific. Include buildings and places of worship. Ask the class what aspects most religions share.

Encourage them to come up with answers such as:
● they all have someone or something that is worshipped
● they have rules of behaviour
● they call for kindness to one's neighbour, help for the poor
● they call for respect and compassion for other people
● they call for respect for parents
● they have goals of peace and justice
● they have buildings for worship (church, mosque, synagogue, gurdwara)

■ If appropriate, ask pupils to put together their views so far about what terrorism is, and whether they think that the groups studied in this Unit were terrorist or not.

Unit 3:
The Jigsaw of Terrorism

KEY VOCABULARY

refugee: a person who leaves home as a result of war or other great difficulty and looks for help and safety in another place

humiliated: made to feel worthless and unimportant

exile: someone who has felt it necessary to leave his/her native country and live abroad

identity: all the different parts of who a person is

identify with: to see oneself as being similar to, or in the same situation as, someone else

rebel: (noun) someone who fights against authority or the people in charge

justify: to try to show that something is right, to give good reasons for something

radical: very different, unusual or extreme

extreme: something or someone that is very different, very strong, very far away, or very unusual compared to others

extremism: very strong views that not many people share, or that not many people think are acceptable or correct

radicalisation: the process by which a person's views become extreme, especially with regard to support for or use of violence

destructive: causing great damage and harm

cease-fire: an agreement, sometimes for a short time only, by both sides of a conflict to stop attacking one another

symbol: an example or picture that represents something

revolution: a time of great change when a government is overturned and a new one takes over

intruder: someone who enters a building unlawfully, often to commit a crime

jihad: in faith terms, a struggle with one's duties, relationships and responsibilities; in a broader sense, a holy war or struggle on behalf of Islam   >>

Aim and content of Unit 3

The aim of Unit 3 is twofold: (1) to help teachers to understand and to explain how and why terrorism occurs, with a particular focus on the process of radicalisation into violence, and (2) to illustrate the consequences of terrorist violence for communities on both sides of a divide.

The Unit begins with a narrative of hate provided by a simple fictional Storyline. This explores the feelings of anger and disappointment and illustrates the causes and consequences of terrorism through the sufferings of one family. The various aspects of terrorism that we need to understand are then introduced as a jigsaw puzzle: we need to find the different sections of the jigsaw and set them into a pattern. Pupils are invited to reflect again on: *reasons* – why terrorists are angry and what their grievances are; *goals* – the rewards that terrorists seek; and *methods* – what terrorists do and to whom – as a means by which we can begin to distinguish terrorism from other kinds of violence. A final section of the jigsaw, which we call *pathways into terrorism*, looks at the drivers and facilitating factors which lead to the leap – taken, relatively speaking, by very few – from anger and grievance to the use of extreme violence.

Unit 3.6, which may be more appropriate for older classes, looks at four contrasting case studies of terrorist violence. In each case reasons, goals and methods are explained clearly and objectively. In three of the four case studies where terrorism has effectively concluded (the exception being Al-Qaeda and Islamic State/ISIS), the factors that brought it to an end are explained.

Finally the Unit draws common threads from the case studies and suggests that whereas there may be a close link between   >>

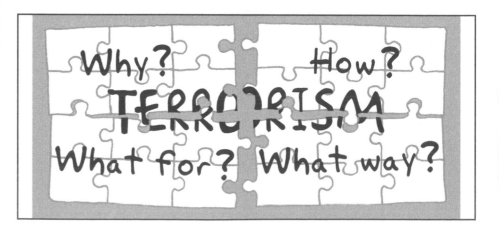

LEARNING OUTCOMES

By the end of Unit 3, pupils will be able to:

■ describe how the destructive force of hatred affects people, and how hate narratives are transmitted through generations

■ distinguish terms such as *extremism* and *radicalisation*, and how they relate to terrorism

■ outline the differences between *reasons, goals* and *methods* of terrorism with reference to contemporary case studies

■ follow different *pathways into terrorism* and the circumstances that influence choices, bearing in mind that the majority of people, even if they have strong grievances, do not take the path of violence

■ explain why calling someone either a terrorist or a freedom fighter is often more a matter of opinion than fact, and why the analysis of *methods* provides a more reliable indicator of terrorism than reasons or goals

■ understand how an individual's perspectives on violence can change with time and experience

■ consider the consequences of terrorist violence: that terrorism destroys lives and communities on both sides of a conflict

KEY VOCABULARY (cont)

ally; allied: a friend or partner, often in a military sense; in a (military) partnership with

civil war: a war fought between rival groups of citizens within the same country

corrupt: to make someone dishonest or wicked

polluted: dirty or harmful to health

overreact: to respond too strongly to something

compromise: an agreement where each side gives up a part of what it wants

common ground: an area that people share, a place where they can agree

consequences: the result or effects of something that has happened earlier

RECOMMENDED MATERIALS

A jigsaw, preferably a simple large one with few pieces, or make one yourself with paper and card. Pupils can then assemble the pieces on a board

Board and white paper on which to illustrate the various stages of the Storyline

Class photocopies of:

• the Storyline (PCM3)

• the school role-play scenarios (PCM4)

Maps of:

• Europe (Ireland and Italy)

• The Middle East (Syria, Iraq)

• Oceania (Papua New Guinea)

religion and terrorism, terrorism derives more from historical and political circumstances than from religious ideology. The case studies show that terrorism frequently ends in stalemate, at which point weariness with violence, plus a recognition on all sides that victory is unobtainable or too elusive, leads finally to compromise and eventual pacification. One case study shows the unique role that women can play in peacemaking.

Notes for teachers

During discussion of the issues raised in this Unit, some pupils might express support for hate narratives and/or express views in favour of violence. Such views should be challenged on the grounds that they are not consistent with school values. Depending on the age of the pupil and the viewpoints expressed, teachers may wish to consult with and seek advice from colleagues. (See also *How to Get the Most from this Handbook*.)

3.1 Introduction

Discuss with pupils how we use a jigsaw. We know that a jigsaw is a complete picture of something, but until we fit all the different pieces together we don't know what the picture shows us. Explain that in this Unit we are going to try to fit together some different sections of the terrorism jigsaw. To begin with, and to help us work out what the jigsaw sections might be, we start with a story – what might be called a narrative of hate.

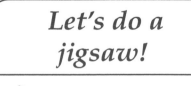

Let's do a jigsaw!

STORYLINE: Bobo – a narrative of hate[29]

PCM3

The scene is a **refugee** camp with tents and tin huts in the (fictional) country of Exland. Bobo – a young boy aged 13 – is listening to his grandfather tell stories of when the family owned a farm with fertile land – a place where they could grow good crops and feed cattle. That was before soldiers from over the border in Wyland invaded Exland and drove the family off their farm. The Wylanders said that Exland had belonged to them two hundred years ago, and so they had a right to take it back. Grandfather, his son Jan, Jan's wife Rena and their two sons, Bobo and his brother Sam, were forced onto a truck with many others and driven for two days to a camp in another part of the country. This camp is close to a city and near a big industrial complex. Jan, Bobo's father, finds a job in a factory but he hates it. He misses the farm. Jan's employers don't respect their workers and treat them badly. Rena, Bobo's mother, has to work as cleaner for a family of rich Wylanders. She grows thin and her hair starts to grey, though she is still quite young. Every day grandfather talks about his hatred for the Wylanders, and his anger and hatred are passed down to Bobo and Sam. Once their family had their own home and they were strong and proud. Now they are hardly surviving.

Sam is 17. He has a job in a market garden, which is between the camp and the city, and to reach it he has to go through a Wyland army checkpoint and show a special pass. He is often searched and the guards enjoy being rude to him, saying insulting things about Exland. Because they are in charge, he cannot say anything, but it makes him furious inside. He feels **humiliated**, as if he counts for nothing and is being crushed into the ground under the heels of the soldiers. Through his work he makes new friends, then he starts to come home very late at night and gradually he stops going to work altogether. He has long conversations on his mobile phone but never tells his family what he is thinking or doing. One day he and a companion throw a home-made bomb at the army checkpoint. The bomb explodes and kills three soldiers, but Sam is killed in the blast as well.

Jan, Rena and Bobo leave the camp in a hurry, bundling grandfather into an old truck, and drive away as fast as possible, afraid of being killed by the soldiers. They manage to get to the coast and from there they take a boat to another country. Here Bobo goes to school and learns a new language, but he finds it hard to settle down or make friends. His life feels very strange, as if it is split in two. When he is at school he is in the new country, but when he is at home with his sad, angry parents, he feels he is back in Exland. Their TV sometimes shows news of Exland, which is still ruled by Wylanders. Life is hard for the Exlanders; they don't have enough to eat and are often treated badly. There have been protests, some of them violent, but they have been put down fiercely. Years pass and Bobo, who is clever at school but can't see any point in studying, gets a job at a building site.

One evening after work he meets two women from Exland who, like him, are **exiles**. One of them is skilled on the computer and has set up a website for people who left after the invasion. The website explains what happened, and shows how badly the Exlanders are being treated. It asks all the exiles to do something to help. The other woman is a very powerful speaker. When she talks at meetings, or even just to Bobo, he feels himself filling up with fire and fury. The women introduce him to other exiles and suddenly Bobo feels he belongs, he has found his **identity**. He **identifies with** this group of people who share his background and his feelings. They argue all the time about what they should do. Sending money is one possibility, but Bobo wants to be involved, he wants to act. He has a goal – he wants the Exlanders to have the right to live freely in their own country again. He wants to be responsible for taking his family home. The two women say that in order to achieve that goal he must go back and attack the Wylanders who occupy Exland. They warn Bobo he might get killed too, like his brother Sam, but he doesn't care. In fact it makes him want to go all the more. Nothing could be more noble than to die like Sam.

Before this time, Bobo had felt lost and without any direction for the future. The two women make him feel proud again, give his life a purpose. They arrange for him to go back secretly to Exland. He says nothing to his family but takes a plane and then a bus and slips across the border. A man is waiting to take him to a training camp in the mountains. There he joins a group of **rebels** and is given a gun. His companions are all from Exland too. They are hard, bitter men. They don't seem interested in freedom and peace, only in money, weapons and winning power for themselves. They want to kill as many Wylander settlers as possible; it doesn't matter if they are women and children. They sell drugs and steal cars – anything to get money and have more power over others in the group. Bobo's group is sent on a mission. They raid a farm (Bobo wonders if it was his grandfather's) and kill everyone on it except a boy aged 10 – Bobo's age when he and his family were driven off their farm. The child is crying and alone. Bobo suddenly wonders what he is doing there. Where has all the hatred led him – just to kill a bunch of farm workers and this boy's family, leaving him alone in the world? An orphan who in turn will carry hatred around all his life. Was this family the enemy? Is violence bringing any good to anyone? Bobo thought he was fighting for a just cause, but now he feels that killing innocent people has turned him into a terrorist.

Bobo leaves his group and goes back across the border, taking the boy with him to his parents' house. They have been worried sick about him. They never imagined that he would go and fight; he always seemed a quiet, peaceful character. They are happy to have him back and to give the little boy a home. Bobo decides there must be a better way to fight than by killing ordinary people. With help and money from local community leaders, Bobo sets up a crafts market where Exlanders can use traditional skills to make products for the local community. The newspapers write about it. Local politicians are interested, and he hopes to speak to a member of the government. The government might then ask the leaders of Wyland to talk about a solution to the problem. Violence cannot be the answer. As Bobo has discovered, terrorism only creates more hatred and more violence.

Make a **diagram of the hate narrative** along the following lines:

INVASION OF EXLAND BY WYLAND
↓
ANGER AND HATRED + DESIRE FOR REVENGE
↓
HATE NARRATIVE GOES DOWN GENERATIONS
↓
HUMILIATION, GRIEVANCES
↓
KILLING OF SOLDIERS, DEATH OF SAM
↓
EXILE
↓
ANGER + HATRED
↓
NEED FOR ACTION, TO FIND AN IDENTITY
↓
OUTSIDE INFLUENCES ENCOURAGE HATRED, DESIRE FOR REVENGE
↓
VIOLENCE CONTINUES
↓
HATE NARRATIVE PASSES TO NEW GENERATION
↓
LIFE IS WORSE FOR EXLANDERS

OR

PEACEFUL ACTIVISM
↓
LIFE IMPROVES FOR EXLANDERS
↓
CHANCE OF PEACEFUL SOLUTION

CLASSROOM/ASSEMBLY ACTIVITY

■ Make a storyboard of the Storyline. Ask pupils to break it down into 6 or 8 sections. Make an illustration for each section and ask pupils to describe in their own words what is happening in each.

■ Discuss the story with the class in its different phases. Focus on the key figures:

Grandfather: who represents history, a storyteller who passes on his anger and hatred to the younger generations

Sam: his personal experiences, actions and death show the effects of humiliation and disrespect, and how these lead to hatred and a desire for revenge

Bobo: split between his old life and his new one; he belongs to neither

The women leaders from Exland: they encourage Bobo to go and fight, giving him a sense of belonging. They convince him that he has a just cause, that violence is right and necessary

The orphan boy: he completes the circle of hatred and may be about to continue it

Ask the class to choose the character they most identify with and write a diary entry for that character. How would they have acted if they had been that character?

3.2 The reasons, or the WHY? of terrorism

Remind the class that we are doing a jigsaw of terrorism. We can call the first section of the jigsaw the *reasons*, or the *Why?* of terrorism. Explain that terrorism has roots, in the same way that plants and trees have roots in the ground. The roots of terrorism are often called *grievances*. Grievances are the *reasons* why terrorists are angry and disappointed, why they think things are unfair, and why they feel hatred for the person or people whom they hold responsible. In their minds, these reasons **justify** violence. They think they have a *just cause*, that using violence is right and revenge is necessary.

Using words carefully

Explain that talking about terrorism is very difficult and we need to choose our words carefully. One problem is that not everyone uses the same words in the same way.

When someone has very strong opinions compared to people around them we might say they have **radical** or **extreme** views. (The word 'radical' comes from the Latin word for a root.) Emphasise that someone can have extreme or radical views but may not be involved in violence at all. Some people whom we might call 'extreme' are simply people who want to excel at something and are fanatical about it, like playing the violin or windsurfing.[30] We talk about 'extreme' sports which only a minority of people do because they are so difficult.

Extremist and **extremism**, as well as *violent extremism*, are words we often hear when terrorism is discussed. We can say that 'extremist' views are ones that not many people share, or that not many people think are acceptable or correct. Having extremist views *can* be limited to opinions, and does not mean that an individual supports or is involved in violence. But it may mean that someone *does not disapprove of the use of violence in certain circumstances*. The problem is that we have no way of knowing what those circumstances might be. If we say that a person supports violent extremism then we can say that he or she has very strong views *and* supports the use of violence to back them up.

The process by which a person develops very strong and extreme opinions which can sometimes – but not always – lead to violence, is called **radicalisation**.

Explain that the words 'radicalised' and 'radicalisation' have taken on a different meaning from the word 'radical'. People are sometimes said to have radical views when their ideas are new, exciting, or very different. Nowadays when we say that someone has been *radicalised* we mean that he or she is likely to be involved in activity that uses or supports terrorism. In the Storyline we could see how Bobo was radicalised.

Suggest that these are very difficult words, and emphasise again that we should take care using them.

Explain that the passing of time does not always make anger and hatred fade away, as the roots and trees example shows. Sometimes it is quite the opposite. It can happen that the stories handed down from grandparents to children and grandchildren about unfairness become even stronger and more important as time goes on. Sometimes the facts become changed as the story continues. Having a very powerful story to believe in about your own people or community can give more meaning to your life. This can be good, but if the story is one of hatred then it can be dangerous and **destructive**.

Ask the pupils if they can think of any stories – happy or unhappy – passed down the generations in their family or community.

Remind pupils that there are different reasons why people feel they are being treated unfairly and humiliated. They may feel that their way of life is being threatened, or that they do not have the freedom to practise their faith or their traditional customs. We saw examples of this in Unit 2. Another reason may be because people cannot live in a

> **TIP**
>
> Ask the class, having studied the story of Bobo and his family, if they can suggest any pieces that make up the Why? section of the terrorism jigsaw. Answers might include:
> - a story passed down through generations of a family or a community keeps anger and hatred going
> - being treated badly can be your own experience or it can be the experience of people you *identify* with
> - people don't usually decide to use violence on their own, other people may encourage them
> - having an enemy can give your life a new purpose or meaning, especially if it felt empty before

particular area that they feel is their homeland. They have no political power and cannot rule themselves in that area.

Sometimes people are angry because of their own experiences of being treated badly, at other times they feel angry *on behalf of others*. Explain that feeling emotions on behalf of someone else is not unusual. Ask the class to think of examples, eg from your classroom window you can see your little sister being teased by another girl. You can do nothing because you are in class, but your anger grows inside you. You feel anger on behalf of your sister. When you finally get outside and find the girl who did the teasing, what would you most like to do? You probably want to get your own back. What *should* you do?

Ask the class to think of other examples, eg supporting a football team. If your team loses and you think the referee's decisions were wrong you might become angry on behalf of your football team. You are not a member of the team and you do not know its members personally, but you feel you belong to it, or identify with it.

Point out that identifying with other people can be a good thing. If we see pictures on TV of the effects of a tsunami, or of people whose homes have been destroyed by an earthquake, we feel sorry for them. We want to help, and sometimes we can.

Ask pupils to think of different ways in which they can help other people who live far away, for example after a natural disaster.

Television and the Internet often show pictures of countries where there is fighting and where people are suffering. If the people who suffer are people of our own community or faith then we may feel particular sympathy for them. We feel that we are all part of the same family, even if they are complete strangers. In some cases this makes people angry and they want to become involved directly, like Bobo did. We cannot say that Bobo was wrong to feel angry, we can understand and perhaps even share his anger.

3.3 The goals, or the WHAT FOR? of terrorism

The second section of the jigsaw includes the *goals*, or the *What for?* of terrorism. Remind the class that terrorists always have *goals*. Goals are the rewards that terrorists (and others) want to win for their group or community. They are *political goals*. If the terrorist group has political goals then it wants political power. Political power gives the group – or the community it represents – the power to decide about important matters like how and where to live, who makes the laws of the land and what sort of laws should be made. These include laws on religious practice and worship. We have seen examples of political goals in Units 1 and 2. The goals for a terrorist group can be called 'long-term', such as winning independence for their people. This is their *ideal*, ie what the terrorists most want. But they can also have 'short-term' goals, such as having companions freed from prison. Long-term goals are the really important ones; short-term goals are staging posts or smaller battles along the way.

Make it very clear to pupils that the majority of people with political goals have nothing to do with terrorism. Having political goals and the wish to have political power are part of our human rights. To reinforce this, ask pupils to discuss the goals they may have.

Despite this, people sometimes make up their minds about whether something is terrorism or not on the basis of goals. If they agree with or share the goals of a particular fighting group they may call its members 'freedom fighters'. If they do not agree with or share the goals, they call its members 'terrorists'. There is a saying, 'One man's terrorist is another man's freedom fighter.' When people use the words 'terrorism' or 'terrorist' they put a label on something. The label says, 'this is bad' or 'these are people we don't like.'

Ask pupils if they think this is a useful way of deciding what terrorism is. Suggest that to call people terrorists because we don't agree with their goals is not a very good way of deciding things. Why? Because these are *opinions*, not *facts*. And we will never reach a universal agreement if we rely on opinions.

Invite pupils to discuss the differences between fact and opinion: eg
'My cat is black with white paws.' Is that fact or opinion?
'I think Kylie Minogue (or someone else) is fantastic.' Is that fact or opinion?
'You're stupid to support that football team because it's useless.' How many facts/opinions are expressed here?

3.4 The methods, or the HOW? of terrorism

Remind pupils that we have been finding the different sections of a jigsaw puzzle of terrorism and putting them together. First of all we found some pieces in the section that we call *reasons*, and then we filled in the part that we call *goals*. They were quite different from each other. Now we have to fill in the pieces we call *methods*. Methods are what terrorists actually do, like shooting or kidnapping people, setting off bombs in public places or blowing up buildings. Terrorist methods, as we have seen, always involve the threat or use of violence. Looking at methods also means thinking about who is affected by violence – the victims of terrorism. Remind the class that the victims of terrorism are usually civilians, ordinary people going about their lives.

Remind pupils about the Suffragettes in Unit 2. Many people agreed with their goals: that women should have the same rights to vote and be members of parliament as men. But some people who had supported the Suffragettes stopped doing so because they disagreed with their methods. They thought using violence was the wrong way to go about things.

In the Storyline, Bobo's goal was to free Exland from the Wyland invaders. Bobo was sincere when he went back to Exland that he wanted to help his country. He also wanted to take revenge for his brother Sam's death. He blamed the Wylanders for it, even though Sam had caused his own death accidentally. But Bobo discovered that his companions were more interested in making money and winning power for themselves than in anything else. They had forgotten the goals of peace and freedom. Bobo found that there was nothing noble or heroic about using violence. When he found he had to kill ordinary people who worked on a farm and that even children were to be killed, he began to question whether killing and injuring civilians was part of a just cause. He felt he was destroying himself as well as other people. He decided that there must be better, non-violent ways of reaching his goal.

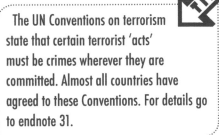

Suggest to the class, or help them to the following conclusion:
People often have good reasons for being angry and disappointed. Often their grievances are real ones. Everyone has the right to want political power and to have political goals. Having reasons and having goals have nothing to do with terrorism if they do not harm other people. But if achieving those goals means destroying the lives of ordinary men, women and children or forcing them to leave their homes then the goal may still be good, but the methods may well be wrong.

Universal agreements on terrorist methods

Explain to the class that it has been impossible to get countries around the world to agree on a definition of terrorism, that is, to agree exactly what terrorism *is*. Why? Because they cannot agree in what circumstances, if ever, using violence is justified and when it is wrong. There are just too many differences of opinion. But they *have* been able to find agreement in an area where facts, not opinions, are what matter. The United Nations has drawn up 14 Conventions or international laws.[31] These Conventions state that certain acts – what we would call terrorist methods – must be thought of as crimes by all the countries that sign the Conventions. Hijacking, hostage-taking, kidnapping, attacks on ships and aircraft and attacks on public buildings, services or public transport are generally agreed to be 'terrorist' because they are deliberately aimed at civilians. Every country must try to arrest and put on trial those responsible so that they cannot avoid punishment by escaping to another country.

The UN Conventions on terrorism state that certain terrorist 'acts' must be crimes wherever they are committed. Almost all countries have agreed to these Conventions. For details go to endnote 31.

CLASSROOM/ASSEMBLY ACTIVITY

PCM4

- In groups of four, ask pupils to select from a set of three role-play cards (PCM4) and act out their scenario to the rest of the group. When the sketch is performed that illustrates 'wrong methods' other pupils in the class should explain why this is so, in contrast to the other two sketches. Feel free to create alternative scenarios based on home or school situations.

3.5 The pathways, or the WHAT WAY? into terrorism

Explain that there is still another section missing in our jigsaw puzzle. We still have to understand more about the process of radicalisation – that is, the pathways that lead an individual to the point where he or she decides to use violence. We have looked at the story of Bobo and we can see why he felt a need to act, and why he thought violence was necessary – he felt it was the only way to help his homeland become free. We know that many people have reasons for being angry and many people have political goals. But compared to all the people in the world who feel angry and disappointed and who have grievances, there are very, very few people who are ready and willing to use terrorism to reach their goals. What makes them different?

Other people

Explain that people become radicalised in many different ways and for each individual the pathway is different. It doesn't usually happen from one day to the next. It almost always involves other people. People hardly ever become radicalised on their own. They may join a group because they have a friend or relation who is already a member. People tend to trust one another more if they have ties of family or friendship, and this is true of terrorists as well.

Shared feelings

Remind the class that there is always a grievance, feelings of anger and a sense that things are unfair. People who join a terrorist group may be unhappy with their lives. They may be bored or lonely, and looking for a more exciting life. They might need something to be involved in, like Bobo. He was lonely and felt he did not belong properly either to his home country or to his new country. He looked for people to share these feelings with and to share an enemy with. He felt stronger and more alive when he shared these feelings.

Violence as 'heroic'

Terrorists sometimes feel themselves to be noble heroes going into battle against a mighty enemy. Tell the class about Anders Breivik, the Norwegian terrorist who killed 77 people in two locations in July 2011. First he set off a home-made car bomb outside the prime minister's office in Oslo, killing 8 people and injuring 200. Then, dressed as a policeman, he crossed over to an island campsite run by the youth branch of the governing Labour party. There he shot dead 69 teenagers and their teachers. At his trial Breivik said he was acting in 'self-defence' and was helping to save Norway's culture and identity. He didn't know or care about his victims, his enemy was the Norwegian government. He said the Norwegian and other European governments were destroying Europe's Christian traditions by allowing mass Muslim immigration. We call this 'right-wing' terrorism: it shares some ideas with Nazism because it often involves racial hatred.

Anders Breivik acted alone but shared his views with others online. He felt stronger because he thought thousands of other people felt the same as he did.

Explain that there are many different pathways into terrorism, perhaps as many as there are terrorists. A variety of factors have to come together. We cannot point to one event or one cause and say 'this is the way' into terrorism. For this reason, explain that we may never know enough about terrorism to complete our jigsaw.

Personal experiences

An individual may choose violence after an experience of members of his/her community being treated badly; a physical or racial attack on someone in the family, community or faith; a personal experience of humiliation or cruelty which turns out to be shared with others. Another important influence could be hearing a powerful speech, connecting to a particular Internet or social media site or meeting a strong or inspiring leader. In Bobo's case many different influences were at work. One of the most important was his meeting with the two women from Exland.

A sea to swim in

Explain that there can be a community of people who support terrorism but do not actively participate in violence. They are rather like a sea, and the terrorists are the fish who swim in it. Terrorists need a sea of supporters for two reasons: (1) because they need people to hide them, give them a place to stay, money, or training in how to carry out attacks, and (2) because they feel stronger when they are members of a group – they encourage and support one another. Being part of something bigger gives them the idea that they are fighting for a good cause. Point out that the sea doesn't necessarily include the families of terrorists. Sometimes they are the last people to know what is going on, like Bobo's parents. In his case the 'sea' was the group of exiles that he met through the two women.

Tell the class about Shehzad Tanweer, one of the four young men who exploded rucksack bombs on three underground trains and a bus on 7 July 2005 in London. The four killed themselves and 52 other passengers. A friend of Shehzad's father said he couldn't understand how the 22-year-old had become involved in terrorism. He said, 'I knew Shehzad: he was very intelligent, normal, polite – nothing to suggest he was a troublemaker. Shehzad's parents really, really looked after him. They gave him everything. He was doing well at university.'[32]

Explain that some individuals find their pathway into violence through the words of a religious text or a religious preacher. They are led to believe that violence will be blessed by the god in whose name they are fighting for a better world. Some believe that their reward will be a place in paradise. But there are many other examples of terrorism that have nothing to do with religion as we have seen. Terrorists may be fighting for an independent homeland or because they are angry about the way their country is run. We will look more closely at real-life examples in the next part.

SUMMARY UNIT 3.1–3.5

Sum up what has been learned so far:

■ It is useful to separate reasons, goals and methods of terrorism. We can understand or agree with the *reasons* why people are angry.

■ We can understand or agree with the *goals* of terrorism. Having reasons and having goals do not make someone a terrorist.

■ When we talk about *methods* we mean what terrorists do, and to whom. These are not opinions but facts. Although there is no agreement on what terrorism is, it is possible to call certain acts 'terrorist'. These acts are ones that involve the deliberate killing or injuring of ordinary people, or civilians.

■ People become radicalised into terrorism for many different reasons, but usually other people are involved in the choice.

■ Terrorists share important beliefs with other people who help them and who support their use of violence. This makes them feel stronger.

> *Let's take a closer look*

3.6 Optional case studies

Use some or all of the following case studies according to their appropriateness for pupils' ages and abilities. Point out on the maps the countries concerned. For younger pupils the Storyline in 3.1 may be sufficient and the case studies can be omitted altogether.

Northern Ireland

Use a map of Western Europe to indicate the location of the island of Ireland, with the Republic of Ireland in the south, and the six counties of Ulster in the north. Explain that Ulster belongs to the United Kingdom. The UK is a monarchy and is ruled by Queen Elizabeth II. Ireland is a separate country and has a president who is elected, not a king or queen.

Explain that terrorism in Northern Ireland has its roots in a quarrel that took place five hundred years ago. It was between King Henry VIII of England, who also ruled over Ireland, and Pope Clement VII, the head of the Catholic Church. After the quarrel (over Henry's wish to end his marriage to Catherine of Aragon and marry Anne Boleyn, which the Pope opposed) Henry said he no longer recognised the authority of the Pope. He named himself as head of the Church of England, divorced Catherine and married Anne. The Church of England became a Protestant church, while the majority of the population in Ireland remained Catholic.

For hundreds of years Catholics in Ireland were unhappy with English and Protestant domination, which discriminated against them. There were battles between Irish rebels and English forces. English lords took over the best land in Ireland. From 1695 and for many years afterwards, laws prevented Catholics from voting, teaching or having professional jobs. When Ireland officially became part of the United Kingdom of Great Britain and Ireland in 1801 many Irish did not want this, and wanted to be independent.

In April 1916 there was a violent protest against the British in Dublin called the Easter Rising. The leaders of the group were arrested, and some were put to death by the British. This led to a bitter struggle for Irish independence from Britain. In 1921 a peace treaty was signed, giving independence to part of Ireland. This later became the Republic of Ireland. Six counties in Northern Ireland, called Ulster, remained British. There was a parliament in Ulster to decide local matters in Northern Ireland, but the British government in London was still in overall charge.

Terrorism started in Northern Ireland because of anger and hatred between two groups – Republicans, who are mostly Catholic, and Unionists, who are mostly Protestant. Republicans want all the people in the island of Ireland to be part of one country and to rule themselves, and Unionists want Ulster to remain part of the United Kingdom.

In the 1960s Catholics who lived in Northern Ireland felt that life was very unfair. In fact Protestants did enjoy more rights and had better housing, schools and jobs. Catholics formed a Civil Rights Association (following the example of Martin Luther King's movement in the US – see Unit 1) to demand equal rights, and held protest marches in towns in Northern Ireland. The Provisional Irish Republican Army – the IRA – was formed in 1969. Its goal was to get rid of British rule in Northern Ireland and to make the whole island of Ireland into one country.

On 30 January 1972, British soldiers opened fire on a crowd of protesters during a civil rights march in a Catholic area of Londonderry, killing 13 men and wounding 13 others, one of whom later died. Six months later, on 21 July, the IRA took revenge by planting 23 bombs in Belfast city centre, of which 19 exploded, killing 9 and wounding 130. Among the dead were several children. These events became known as Bloody Sunday and Bloody Friday. The year

> If appropriate explain that: Catholics and Protestants are all Christians, but they follow Christianity in different ways. One difference is that Catholics consider the Pope to be the head of the Church, whereas Protestants do not recognise his authority.

1972 was the worst of the conflict, with 497 people killed, over half of whom were civilians. The violence continued for many more years.

Unionist terrorist groups were also formed, such as the Ulster Volunteer Force and the Ulster Defence Association. Their goal was to keep Ulster united to Britain. They murdered members and supporters of the IRA, and sometimes murdered people just because they were Catholics. The IRA were fighting the Unionists *and* the British security forces. Over 3,000 people were killed between 1969 and the middle of the 1990s. About two thirds were killed by the IRA, one third by Unionist terror groups.

After 30 years of violence, most people in Northern Ireland longed for peace. The armed groups on both sides began to realise that violence had brought no reward but great suffering to both communities. In 1998 there was an important agreement. It is called the Good Friday Agreement because it was signed in Belfast on the Friday before Easter. It said that the Republican and Unionist armed groups would agree to a **cease-fire**. That means they agreed not to carry out further attacks. Then they promised to get rid of all their weapons. In return, British soldiers would no longer patrol the streets of Northern Ireland. The agreement set up a new Assembly (or parliament) for Ulster where Catholic and Protestant political parties share political power. The agreement also says that Northern Ireland will stay British only for as long as most of its people want this. If one day most people in Northern Ireland want to join the rest of Ireland in one country, they can. The violence has not stopped altogether, but peace has more or less returned to Northern Ireland. Unionists and Republicans still disagree about many issues. Anger and hatred have not disappeared. Neither side has given up its goals. But a majority of people on both sides agree that violence is not the way to achieve them.

The Red Brigades, Italy

Ask pupils what comes to mind when they think of Italy. They will probably give examples like football, spaghetti, pizza, etc. These examples of Italy can also be called **symbols**. Some people might say that a symbol of violence in Italy is the Mafia. Explain that the Mafia is certainly a violent group, and its members often terrorise people. But they don't want rewards for other people; they want money and power just for themselves.

Explain that the Red Brigades was the name of a terrorist group in Italy in the 1970s–80s. People joined it because they were angry at the way things were run in Italy, and they wanted to change things. The Red Brigades wanted to start a **revolution**. A revolution is a bit like a war. It happens when the government of a country is overturned and a new one takes over. A revolution usually involves people being killed and injured.

Illustrate the idea of revolution with a group of people breaking down the door of a house and forcing their way inside. The **intruders** throw all the chairs and tables about and break everything they can find. The people who live there try to stop them but they are pushed outside and either killed or sent away. The new people are now in charge and tell everyone what to do.

This is what happens to a country when there is a revolution: everything is turned upside down and topsy-turvy.

Explain that the Red Brigades hated the people who were in charge of the government in Italy and they hated the people who ran big companies and factories. They said that ordinary working people, especially factory workers, were treated like slaves, and worked only to make money for the rich people who owned the factories. They said everyone should share the money equally, and that ordinary working people should be in charge of Italy. They said judges and police officers were particular enemies because they made Italians obey laws that the Red Brigades thought were unfair.

Italy is a democracy – a country where all adults can vote for the political party of their choice. But the Red Brigades knew they would never win enough votes in parliament to govern Italy, so they tried to change things with violence. They tried to terrorise the people in charge of things. They killed, injured and kidnapped politicians, factory managers, judges and policemen. These people were all *symbols* of what they hated. They murdered around 150 people and injured hundreds more. Each time they shot someone they sent a message to newspapers explaining their reasons. The Red Brigades wanted to persuade the Italians that Italy was ruled by bad people and bad laws. They hoped that the Italian population would support them in making a revolution.

Tell pupils about the kidnap of Aldo Moro in 1978. Aldo Moro was a very important politician who had been prime minister of Italy. The Red Brigades shot dead his five bodyguards in a car ambush in the centre of Rome. Then they took Aldo Moro away and kept him hostage in a secret place for almost two months. They wanted to force the government to make a bargain with them: they said they would release their prisoner if the government released some of their companions from prison. What they really wanted was for the government to talk to them as if they were a political party. When the government refused to make a bargain, the Red Brigades killed their hostage. Eventually most Italians said the Red Brigades' violence was wrong. The Italians wanted change but they didn't want a violent revolution. The Red Brigades didn't have any 'sea' to swim in because no one would help them, and most of them were arrested.

Explain if appropriate: The members of Al-Qaeda and ISIS belong to the Sunni branch of Islam. The main difference with Shia Muslims is over who should lead the Islamic faith. Sunnis believe there should be an elected leader or *caliph* whereas Shia followers think that leadership comes down through the family of the Prophet Muhammad and through imams – like priests – who are specially blessed and chosen by the Prophet.

Al-Qaeda and Islamic State

Al-Qaeda and Islamic State (IS) or ISIS – Islamic State in Iraq and Syria – are violent organisations that claim to act in the name of Islam. They are sometimes called *jihadist* groups because their members believe they are fighting a **jihad** or holy war on behalf of their faith. Explain that we call them *umbrella organisations* because each consists of networks of individuals and groups with different leaders in different countries under an 'umbrella' of shared goals. Al-Qaeda in Arabic means 'the base', and Al-Qaeda says it wants to be the base, or starting point, for an Islamic revolution. One of the goals of this revolution is to have Islamic law, called *Sharia*, as the only set of laws that Muslim people obey. These laws would be followed very strictly. Al-Qaeda and ISIS believe democracy is a bad way of government because it depends on laws made by man and not by God. They think that to separate them, as happens in western democracies, is wrong and is a bad way to run a country. Many devout Muslims also believe that religion and law should not be separated. But most Muslims do not support Al-Qaeda or ISIS; they respect and want to live in peace with other religions and communities.

ISIS started as a branch of Al-Qaeda in Iraq, where it fought against the occupation of Iraq by the United States and other **allied** forces in 2003. Another branch started in Syria during the **civil war** there which began in 2011. The two branches then joined forces and became a rival of Al-Qaeda. Disagreements arose between ISIS and Al-Qaeda, mainly over how Islamic law should be followed.

Despite these differences, some of the goals of Al-Qaeda and ISIS are the same. They want:

● to have all Muslims living in a single Muslim community, or *caliphate*, with a leader called a caliph. This would involve the creation of a huge Islamic state covering many countries

● to get rid of westerners and western influences (especially American) from all Muslim countries around the world

● to defeat all those whom they consider to be the enemies of Islam. Among them are the rulers of several Muslim countries, considered enemies because they do not apply Sharia law strictly enough

Al-Qaeda and ISIS consider the United States and its allies as enemies. This is for a number of reasons:

(1) The US led the invasion of Afghanistan in 2001 and of Iraq in 2003, and with its allies occupied these countries for several years, resulting in the death and injury of many thousands of Muslims. Al-Qaeda and

ISIS say that *this* is terrorism. American and allied soldiers continue to have military bases in many Muslim countries.

(2) The US supports Israel, and Israel is seen as a major enemy of Islam. Israel occupies land that Muslims say should belong to the Palestinians. Many Muslims have been killed by Israeli forces in the Palestinian territories. (Israelis have of course also been killed by Palestinian bombers and suicide bombers.)

(3) Al-Qaeda and ISIS believe that the US and its supporters are fighting a war against Islam, and want to destroy it. They believe their duty is to save Islam and keep it pure, and say this is the real meaning of *jihad*. In their view western societies want to **corrupt** Muslims. That means they want to make Muslims dishonest and wicked, and not respect Islamic laws. These organisations think the Islamic way of life is being threatened and that Muslim countries must defend themselves by attacking. Their leaders say that Muslims have a duty to attack Americans – soldiers as well as ordinary American citizens – and citizens of any country that supports America. ISIS has also made threats against Rome, the centre of world Christianity.

On 11 September 2001, 19 members of Al-Qaeda hijacked four planes after take-off in the United States. Two of the planes were deliberately flown into the Twin Towers of the World Trade Center in New York which collapsed, one was crashed into the Pentagon (US Defense headquarters) near Washington and another crashed in a field in Pennsylvania. Around 3,000 people were killed.

ISIS is more violent than Al-Qaeda with regard to other Muslims. Its followers murder Shia Muslims and other Sunni Muslims if they do not agree with ISIS, as well as members of other faith groups in Syria and Iraq. Sometimes whole villages and communities have been murdered. ISIS has also kidnapped and brutally murdered hostages from the UK, the US, Japan and Jordan and posted videos of the killings on the Internet.

The 9/11 and the Paris attacks are discussed further in Unit 4.

Explain that two terrorist attacks in Paris in January 2015 against a magazine and a Jewish supermarket may have been carried out on behalf of both Al-Qaeda and ISIS.

Bougainville, Papua New Guinea

Bougainville is an island in the Pacific Ocean north-east of Australia and is part of the state of Papua New Guinea. After World War 2, Papua New Guinea was ruled by Australia before becoming independent in 1975. But the people of Bougainville felt quite separate from the rest of the country: they were almost 1,000 kilometres from the capital, Port Moresby; they had a different culture and spoke different languages. In 1964 an international mining company discovered precious minerals on the island. Over the next 10 years, the world's biggest copper mine was created at Panguna in southeast Bougainville. To make way for the mine, many thousands of people had to move from their homes. Villages, coconut palms and agricultural land were destroyed, and rivers and streams in the area became **polluted**.

The change to their way of life was felt especially by the women of Bougainville, who by tradition own the land and pass it on to their children. Although they received some money in payment for the land they felt the loss deeply. Thousands of new jobs were created when the mine was built but most of them went to workers from other parts of Papua New Guinea and from Australia, and not to local people. The local people who did work at the mine were paid lower wages than those who arrived from outside, and the mining company took the profits without making life better for the population.

Protests began over how the mine was run, and over the unfair treatment of the Bougainville people. The protesters felt they were not being listened to and their unhappiness grew. They were angry not just about the mine but about how Bougainville was run. They didn't trust the government officials and many felt that Bougainville should be independent of Papua New Guinea.

In 1988 a mineworker called Francis Ona stole explosives from the mine, and, together with others, blew up a power generator. After that they blew up some of the huge electricity pylons that carried power to the mine. These were acts of sabotage, to make it impossible to run the mine. The government in Port Moresby sent in the military to round up the troublemakers and stop the protest. Francis Ona formed the Bougainville Revolutionary Army to fight the government. Its goal was independence from Papua New Guinea.

The mine was closed down because of the attacks against it, and the island was occupied by police and army forces. Then the government authorities made a big mistake. They **overreacted** to the attacks at the mine. This sometimes happens when governments respond to terrorism: it means they used as much or even more violence than the rebels. The military beat up ordinary people and put them in prison without any proof of their guilt. They destroyed homes and farms. They tortured and shot people without trial. Many hundreds of people were sent to so-called 'care centres' which were like prison camps.

During 1990–91 the government of Papua New Guinea declared a State of Emergency and stopped all air and sea traffic from reaching the island. Most public officials and people who were not from the island left. Banks, offices and health services were closed down. No one from outside really knew what was going on. The violence continued: different groups of Bougainvilleans then began to fight each other because they had different goals. The military continued to carry out attacks and the Revolutionary Army killed many soldiers in attacks and ambushes. Thousands of Bougainvilleans were killed or forced to leave their homes, and many starved.

Several times during the early 1990s, peace efforts were made but they all broke down and more violence followed. In 1995 a local government was set up to help solve the conflict. It was led by Premier Theodore Miriung. He tried to bring the different groups together but he was assassinated in 1996.

By 1997 most people in Bougainville were tired of the violence and wanted peace. Their homes, land, family life and work had been ruined. A whole generation of children had not gone to school. Because of the tradition in Bougainville that 'women are mothers of the land', women's groups were especially important in restarting the peace efforts. The women tried to convince the fighting groups to live and work together for a better future.

Another important partner in the peace process was a government that was not directly involved in the conflict. New Zealand Foreign Minister Don McKinnon arranged for talks to take place in New Zealand. To begin with only Bougainvilleans were invited, because first they had to make peace among themselves. Being away from home was helpful. They attended Maori ceremonies and heard about the struggle of the Maoris to have their language and culture recognised in New Zealand.

The next talks involved the Papua New Guinea national government. After this there was a proper timetable for peace. An agreement signed by all sides in 1998 said there would be no more fighting, and made arrangements for how peace could be kept. The rebels agreed to hand in their weapons. The government agreed to give the people of Bougainville much more say in how the island should be run. The agreement said that a referendum would be held between 2015 and 2020 that would allow all adult members of the population to vote on whether they wanted independence.

As happened in Northern Ireland, the agreement did not give any one group exactly what they wanted immediately. It was a **compromise**. But there was enough **common ground** to make it possible to reach an agreement. No one achieved all their goals, but everyone achieved something

Case study discussion suggestions
Encourage pupils to say what if anything the case studies have in common. Take them back to the cooking pot of terrorism ingredients

given in Unit 1: the use or threat of violence to cause terror, usually by *non-state* individuals or groups, ie, not acting for a state or country; grievances (feelings of anger, disappointment and hatred) that are blamed on an enemy and the desire for revenge; the use of violence against 'ordinary people' or civilians; goals of political power that are not just for one person but for a community; the belief that violence is the only way to reach the goals; the aim of attracting as much attention, or publicity, as possible; the aim of sending a message to change the behaviour of an authority or the people in charge.

The four case studies help us to understand the causes of terrorism but they also tell us about the **consequences** of terrorism, the effects that terrorism has on people. Ask pupils what they think is the most important effect of terrorism. Encourage them towards the idea that suffering is the most important. People suffer on all sides of a conflict because attacks by one side lead to 'tit for tat' revenge attacks by the other; violence causes more violence, more hatred and more suffering.

SUMMARY UNIT 3

Suggest some other conclusions that can be drawn from the Storyline and the case studies:

■ History and storytelling can be important elements that keep terrorism going from generation to generation.

■ The reasons for terrorism often have a connection to religion. But religion is usually less important than history and geography: that is, who rules a country, where its borders are, and whether all sections of the population have equal rights.

■ Grievances are felt particularly strongly when outsiders who have authority over a local population discriminate against the local people and treat them without respect.

■ Once terrorism starts it is very difficult to stop because violence rolls forward like a wave. Terrorism creates more terrorism unless people decide together to look for peace.

■ An important consequence of terrorism is that people suffer on all sides of a conflict. Terrorists sometimes come to realise that using violence destroys them and their own community as well as their enemies.

■ Peace has a good chance when everyone is tired of violence and neither side can see victory in sight.

>>

- Women can play a vital role in the peace process.

- Terrorism rarely achieves the goals that terrorists want.

CLASSROOM/ASSEMBLY ACTIVITY

- Encourage pupils to discuss the ways in which arguments can finish peacefully, using everyday situations, such as a dispute about who should play in which part of the playground or yard, or what kind of games or activities are played. The idea of a referee can be introduced – someone who stands between two groups that disagree and who can help to solve a problem. (The analogy with football may be useful.)

- Choose a controversial local or school issue and have the class speak for and against different points of view. Each class can select an issue or a different viewpoint and present these in assembly.

- Invite pupils to write a letter to a member of a terrorist group. The letter could include questions about why the members are angry or what their goals are. Or the letter could simply express what the pupil, or group of pupils, feels about terrorism. It could take the form of, 'I understand you feel that this land is your own, but …'

Unit 4:
Terrorism and the Media

KEY VOCABULARY

mass media: means of communication, news and information such as newspapers, TV, radio and Internet that are open to very large numbers of people. Often shortened to media

communication: a way of being in touch with people or sharing messages

bias; biased: a preference or favour for one side rather than another; being in favour of one side rather than another

live: something that we see happening at the exact moment that it happens

performance: a show or public display

audience: those who listen to or watch a performance

define: to give all the information about what something/someone is

recruit: to persuade someone to join a group or organisation

propaganda: information or ideas, usually exaggerated or misleading, to help a political cause

gag: literally a piece of cloth that covers the mouth and prevents someone from speaking – here referring to something that prevents the media from speaking

censorship: the refusal to allow something to be written or talked about

mouthpiece: a spokesperson, someone who represents the views of a person or group

negotiator: a person who makes a bargain or agreement

Aim and content of Unit 4

The aim of Unit 4 is to explain the role of the mass media and social media networks in the context of terrorism. Journalists are first and foremost storytellers: they give us accounts of world and local events and can contribute greatly to an understanding of conflict. They can explain the background to a community's grievances and how these have evolved into terrorism. Choices of tone and language made by journalists in how they report on terrorism may be a primary influence on public opinion, and this confers particular responsibilities.

Journalists have an important role in shaping the views and perceptions of different sectors of the population, both in terms of how different groups see themselves and how they perceive others. They can also reinforce, or alternatively disrupt, negative stereotypes of minority groups. Internet and electronic media have been used by those who wish to promote hatred, recruit followers to a cause and encourage violence. Social networks operate on a more personal basis than mass media and can be carefully targeted at a particular age group, audience or individual. Social networking sites are easily accessible to young age groups and are difficult to regulate. Unit 4 helps teachers to raise awareness in pupils of the harmfulness of unbalanced media reports and of the need to evaluate sources of online information. It also examines the right to freedom of expression, and what limits, if any, this should have. >>

Reporting on terrorism – finding the balance

LEARNING OUTCOMES

By the end of Unit 4, pupils will be able to:

- explain the role of the media as news gatherers and givers and show that the media are a means of enabling *information*, *communication* and *sharing* at many different levels
- distinguish between *fact* and *opinion* in journalism and recognise *bias* and *propaganda*
- present different sides of a story, and explain why it is important to have a fair and balanced approach to news coverage
- explain why terrorism is a form of performance, and distinguish *victims* from the *target* and the *audience* of terrorism
- describe the symbolic value of a terrorist attack
- examine how the mass media and social networks interact with terrorism, and how information can be manipulated to cause fear and hatred
- consider the dilemmas surrounding censorship, and debate what limits there should be, if any, on the freedom of expression
- describe the role of negotiation and bargain-making with terrorists, and the risks of media involvement in this area
- recognise the qualities that are necessary for a good journalist and how journalism can contribute to conflict resolution, the overcoming of negative images in popular media and the promotion of human rights. They will conclude that journalism in this area is an extremely difficult profession

RECOMMENDED MATERIALS

Computers (if available)

Newspapers, local and national

Photo images of:

- the Twin Towers of the World Trade Center in New York after the 9/11 attacks
- a tightrope walker

Terrorists want publicity above all else and use violence as a means of forcing the media to communicate their message. They try to subvert the media to achieve other goals, in particular to influence public and government opinion to grant concessions. Journalists may become participants or direct interlocutors with whom terrorist groups try to negotiate advantages for themselves. The Unit concludes with a summary of the importance and the risks of journalism.

Notes for teachers

This Unit gives particular opportunities for class activities and debate. A short play could also be staged set around a newsworthy story. Encourage pupils to bring in news stories or other sources of news and information.

4.1 Who are the media and what do they do?

Ask pupils how they receive news, starting with news about family and friends, and then about the wider world. Discuss the difference between local news, national news and international news. Ask them to give examples of what kind of information comes from each. Give pupils some headings from newspapers or the Internet. Ask them to sort them into the categories of local/national/international

Let's talk about the media

news. (Some may be a combination of all three, eg the 2014 *Tour de France* which began in Yorkshire.)

Explain that the main sources of news like newspapers, radio, TV and Internet are called the **mass media**. They are called this because they are available to masses of people. We often shorten this word to simply **media**.

Explain that these are all types or channels of **communication**. Discuss with the class the different roles of television, radio, newspapers, Internet sites like YouTube, and social media networks such as Twitter, Facebook, etc. Emphasise their function as sources of *information, communication* and *sharing*. Discuss these three words and what they signify.

Suggest that we can communicate or share things in many different ways without words. Write on a board or on small slips of paper some wordless communication activities for pupils to act out: eg

- someone expressing joy at the result of a football match or other sporting game

- a child running up to another and spontaneously hugging him/her

- someone receiving a letter through the post and expressing great joy/distress

- sign language used by people who cannot hear or speak

- body language that tells us when someone is afraid, angry, etc

Remind the class about the discussion on rights from Unit 1. Suggest that having rights often goes together with having responsibilities. Ask them (briefly) what sort of responsibilities parents and teachers have, and what responsibilities young people have. Explain that journalists or reporters – the people who give us the news – also have responsibilities. Invite pupils to say what they think these are. Encourage them towards the idea that journalists should *try to tell the truth* and *give the facts*. Explain that this is not as easy at it sounds. Journalists talk to many different people and they all have different views and different experiences. There are many different ways to tell a story, and the same story will change with each person you talk to. Journalists need to know a lot of background before they can tell a story correctly. They have to do homework too!

For younger age groups: Ask pupils to think of a story that they know very well such as the story of the Big Bad Wolf and the Three Little Pigs. The story has been rewritten from the Wolf's point of view.[33]

> **TIP** What form of information, communication or sharing is involved with each of the different types of media? What differences are there between them? (Eg Instagram is especially intended for photo exchange, tweets are limited to 140 characters, and YouTube is used for video- and music-streaming.)

This time the story is that the Wolf runs out of sugar to make his grandmother a birthday cake. He has a bad cold and when he goes to borrow sugar from the Little Pigs he sneezes all over their houses and they fall down. It's all an accident and he isn't such a bad Wolf after all.

An alternative character to illustrate this point is Severus Snape from the Harry Potter series. In the first books Snape is shown as cruel and a bully, someone who hates Harry. Only much later in the series do we learn that he was bullied by Harry's father at Hogwarts and that he was in love with Harry's mother. We also learn that he was not Harry's enemy but was trying to protect him from Voldemort. We only knew part of Snape's story in the early books, we didn't have all the facts.

Take pupils back to the subject of bullying. It is possible to write a story about bullying in which the victim of bullying is nothing but good and the person doing the bullying all bad. But the truth might be that the person doing the bullying had an unhappy time at home, and that other people had been cruel to him or her. Being cruel to someone else can seem like a way of coping. This doesn't change the fact that bullying is unacceptable behaviour. But it helps us to understand why the behaviour happened. It changes the way the story is written. To write a story that is truthful and fair you have to know the facts.

> Choose an alternative fable or story if you wish as appropriate.

CLASSROOM/ASSEMBLY ACTIVITY

- Ask pupils to imagine that a reporter from a local paper has written a newspaper article about their school. She never once came to the school and didn't talk to the teachers or to the pupils. Her article was full of mistakes. That was not responsible behaviour, because she didn't bother to find out the facts. Ask the class to prepare two different versions of the article, one true and one false.

- Ask a colleague or a pupil to enter the classroom after the lesson has started and announce that something strange or exciting has happened (eg someone is trapped in a tree, has gone missing or a crime has taken place). Ask pupils to create an 'incident scene' writing down all the facts as they are known. Pupils will discover what they judge to be important information and what not.

4.2 Fact, opinion and bias

Remind pupils about the difference between fact and opinion (Unit 3). Suggest that both facts and opinions can be interesting, but it is necessary to separate the two.

> Ask the class quickly to think of five facts and five opinions.

Choose an alternative competition as appropriate.

Remind the class that during the 2014 World Cup in Brazil, the football matches were watched all over the world. TV cameras and journalists from all the countries that took part were in Brazil to report on their teams. When England played Italy on 14 June the match that was shown on TV was the same match, wherever in the world it was watched. (*Result: Italy 2, England 1*)

Ask pupils if there was a difference between watching the match in Italy and watching it in England. Point out (if necessary) that the journalist who worked for Italian TV spoke in Italian for all the people watching the match in Italy. The journalist who worked for British TV spoke in English for all the TV viewers in Britain.

Ask pupils if they can think of any other differences. Suggest that the two journalists wanted a different result from the match. Both of them hoped that their own country's team would win. Each was **biased** in favour of his own country. That means the Italian journalist shouted for joy when Italy scored a goal; the English journalist did the same when England scored. The referee was neither English nor Italian. Why? Because he might have been biased in favour of his own country. The Dutch referee had a more *balanced* view.

Lead the class into a discussion of what it means to be biased – to be in favour of one side rather than another. Remind them that even if sports journalists are biased they still have a responsibility to report the facts. In other words, when Brazil lost 1–7 to Germany no Brazilian reporter could say that the Brazilian team had played well.

Point out that reporting on terrorism on TV, radio and newspapers is very difficult, much more difficult than reporting on a football match. Ask the class why this should be.

They could answer by saying that a football match does not usually involve people being killed or seriously injured, unlike terrorism. We could also say that football is a game that has rules (even if players do not always obey them!) A referee makes sure that the rules are respected. With terrorism there are no rules and a terrorist attack is always a surprise. At first we often do not know who has done what, or why. The media are much more important here because we need them to tell us what has happened.

Explain that, as with a football match, the story will be presented differently depending on where the journalist lives. Reporting on terrorism often contains bias, depending on who is hurt, who the terrorists are (or are thought to be) and where the terrorist attack takes place. Obviously, the people who will be most affected by the terrorist attack are those in the places where the victims and their families come from. Journalists in these places still have a responsibility to report the facts of what has happened. But they will naturally have a bias – they will feel particular sympathy and concern for the victims, and particular fury at the terrorists. These feelings will change the way they write. It is difficult to be balanced in this situation. Professional journalists usually try to be balanced, but passers-by who use their smartphones to film and post their accounts on social networks have no responsibility to tell the truth. We should always hear different points of view, and someone should always say, 'Hey, wait a minute, isn't there another side to this story?'

CLASSROOM/ASSEMBLY ACTIVITY

■ Ask the class to look at a newspaper or online article about a conflict. Ask them to identify elements such as fact, opinion and bias. Is more than one side of the story presented? What does the story make them feel?

4.3 Terrorism as performance

Explain that when there is a terrorist attack, TV shows what has happened around the world. Video footage presents the scene of a terrorist attack **live** just as it happens. Film shows the victims' shock and terror and brings their emotions into our lives. It also shows how much damage has been done and how badly hurt the victims are. As we have learned already, this is exactly what terrorists want: to create terror in the population.

For this reason we say that terrorism is a kind of **performance**. Usually we think of a performance as being a concert, a film or a play. Terrorists want an **audience** for their performance, and TV makes it possible to have an audience all over the world.

Point out that the idea of violence as a performance goes back centuries. Remind the class about the Assassins (Unit 2), who always tried to assassinate their victims in a busy public place, usually on a holiday. They wanted as many people as possible to see what they had done. The people who saw the attack would be terrorised even if they were not actually hurt.

Remind the class about the Suffragettes, and how they wanted attention. They wanted everyone to know about them and what they did; they wanted to be 'in the news'. The bolder and more daring the Suffragettes were, the more people paid attention to them. There were no TV or radio at that time but there were cameras and newspapers. The Assassins and the Suffragettes were putting on a performance for an audience.

TIP

Explain that this effect is even greater when terrorists attack *symbols*. Remind the class what a symbol is, eg Unit 3: the Red Brigades attacked symbols of the Italy they hated such as politicians, judges, factory managers.

Point out that because of live TV and video footage on the Internet, the audience for terrorism now includes the whole world. Introduce the idea of an echo: if you go into a cave or tunnel and shout your name it comes back bigger and louder than before. Or imagine a flat, calm pond. If you throw a stone into the water, ripples spread right across the pond. This is what TV and the Internet do for terrorism. They make an echo bigger and louder; they carry the ripples all the way across the world.

Remind pupils of the Al-Qaeda attacks in September 2001. Hijackers took over four planes and made them crash with everyone on board. Two of them were flown into the Twin Towers of the World Trade Center in New York which then collapsed. One was flown into the Pentagon, the headquarters of the United States Defense Department. The fourth crashed into a field when passengers tried to fight the hijackers. The Twin Towers were a famous *symbol* of the city and of the United States. Tourists visiting the US sent home postcards of the Statue of Liberty in New York harbour, with the Twin Towers in the background. They were part of the skyline of the most famous city in the world. Many of the offices in the Towers belonged to important banks and financial companies, so the Towers were also a symbol of wealth in the richest country in the world.

Al-Qaeda had succeeded in their goal: they had killed a lot of Americans (as well as people from many other countries) and they had destroyed *symbols* of America's wealth and power. They had also caused terror in countries across the world.

OPTIONAL ACTIVITY FOR OLDER PUPILS

Suggest that if journalists pay too much attention to the symbol they may forget the suffering of the victims. Tell pupils about two attacks in Nairobi, Kenya, and Dar es Salaam, Tanzania in 1998 by an Al-Qaeda group. The terrorists bombed the US embassies in the two countries because they were a symbol of the United States. Many people saw this as the most important aspect of the attack. In fact almost all the victims were local people who worked in the embassies. In Nairobi, 213 people were killed; 200 of them were Kenyans; 4,000 were injured, nearly all of them Kenyans too. In Dar es Salaam, 11 people were killed, all of them Tanzanian. Yet this was called 'an attack on the United States'.

Suggest that when journalists report on terrorism they have to choose their words very carefully. Ask pupils why this is so. Reasons could include: >>

- If they talk too much about symbols they may forget who the victims are.

- If they use expressions like 'the city is in complete chaos', 'the country is on its knees', or 'the terrorists have scored a victory', this will give the terrorists encouragement.

- If they say too much about the horror of the attack and the emotions of the people involved they may make the population (the audience) even more frightened.

- If they give opinions without knowing the facts they can spread wrong information. This can make things worse and put other people in danger.

- If they write things that the terrorists don't like they risk being killed themselves.

4.4 The terrorist message

Remind pupils that the people who are hurt in a terrorist attack are the *victims of terrorism*. Terrorists always have a *message,* and this is mainly directed at the people in charge. The message is not just, 'We hate you!' or 'We are very angry!' It also says, 'We blame you for all the bad things that have happened to us, which is why we have carried out this attack. Now we want you to change the way you do things!' This might mean changing the way a country is run, changing its laws; bringing soldiers back from a country where they are fighting; or allowing prisoners from the terrorist group to leave prison.

Explain that what is important here is that *terrorists are trying to change people's behaviour*. The people whose behaviour the terrorists most want to change – usually the government or the people in charge – are called the *target*. The target is the person or people who have the power to change the way a country or region is run. Discuss the word target and what it means to the class.

Imagine a game of darts or an archery competition.

Encourage the class to discuss the idea of changing people's behaviour and to think of examples closer to home.

Take the class back to the Storyline in Unit 1 and the kidnap of Rachel Brown. Remind pupils that her kidnappers were not trying to change *her* behaviour – she was just a baby. The person whose behaviour they wanted to change was her father, Elliot Brown. Rachel was the *victim*. Mr Brown was the *target*. The *message* was for him because he was the owner of the building company. He was the one who had the power to change things. The message was, 'You can have your baby back if you agree not to build the shopping centre!' In this case the *audience* was all the inhabitants of Bowmarket. They saw what Ben, Amy and John had done and they decided that it was wrong to kidnap a baby even if the goal was a good one. They stopped supporting the Save Riverside Group.

> **OPTIONAL INFORMATION FOR OLDER PUPILS**
>
> Explain that this leads to another important point. The audience for terrorism is worldwide, but the audience in the country where an attack has happened is particularly important. As we know, terrorists have grievances for which they blame governments or other authorities. In a democracy, adults vote for the government that they want, so terrorists also blame the citizens of a democratic country for what the government of that country does. This is how they 'justify' killing ordinary people. They want the citizens to say to the government: 'We don't like what you're doing either so we also think you should stop it!'

4.5 The media and positive messages

Good journalists understand how vital it is to be able to speak the truth about what is happening in the world. They recognise the importance of human rights, and how these suffer at times of conflict. Tell the class that a Canadian organisation called Journalists for Human Rights (JHR) helped to train journalists in Ghana in how to report human rights stories. As a result the number of media stories about human rights in Ghana went up by two thirds in just a few years. It was actually possible to measure the effect of this on crime in Ghana: certain kinds of crime went down, especially those against girls and women. JHR said it had chosen Ghana because of its growing culture of rights and because journalists were free to write about human rights without interference. This had not been the case in the past.[34]

Writers and journalists can also influence popular opinion. Tell the class about the American Muslim writer, G. Willow Wilson. She felt that the image of Muslims in the media was often negative, and that this image was encouraging hostility and suspicion. She invented the comic book character Kamala Khan, a 16-year-old Pakistani-American girl living with her family in New Jersey.[35] After going to a party without her parents' permission Kamala becomes lost in clouds of mist and emerges with super-powers as *Ms Marvel.* She is a good Muslim but this does not **define** her life and her identity. She's a nerd who writes fanfiction and argues with her parents. Her story is both funny and respectful of Islam, and gives Muslims a positive place in pop culture. The series is hugely popular in the US where it has won almost every award in the comic book industry. The success of the character has helped to change people's ideas about Muslims in a positive way.[36]

Most people would agree that the Internet and social media have had a good impact on our lives. Ask pupils to identify the different aspects of the Internet, eg chat rooms, Facebook, blogs, etc, as appropriate. Explain that the Internet can help us to communicate and to build bridges between ourselves and other people. We can have online friendships and chat to one another through Skype; we can exchange music, play chess, share photos or videos even when we don't know one another in person and live far apart. When we communicate with people whose lives are very different to our own, we find a part of their identity that we share, like an interest in football or a kind of music. When we do this it shows that people who are different can still have many things in common.

Point out that TV, the Internet and social networks can also be useful in fighting terrorism. Not fighting in the physical sense, but in the sense of fighting the idea that violence is the right way to solve problems. Journalists can explain that certain messages only give one side of a story, and that people who stir up hatred and violence are not actually helping the people they want to help, but are making things worse. Journalists often have experience of war and terrorism, and they know how much suffering they cause. Because they travel a lot they meet a wide range of people and can help us to understand why terrorism occurs in different places. Most of all they are storytellers, and can relate in words and pictures how people live and the problems they have. They can show many different points of view and allow different voices to be heard. If they explain the problems of a particular group of people and why they are angry, they may draw the government's attention to their problems. The government may be able to listen to the group's grievances and change things before terrorism starts.

4.6 The media and negative messages

Remind the class that Twitter, YouTube, Facebook and other forms of social media are quite new ways of communicating and sharing. Although many people now depend on them, and they have many good uses, they have also been used to **recruit** young people to join violent organisations. Terrorists use the Internet and social networks to win sympathy and support, to make people feel angry and to send messages that encourage violence. The word sometimes used to describe this is **propaganda**, which means information or ideas that tend to be exaggerated or misleading. Whereas newspapers and TV give different viewpoints, on the Internet it is hard to know what is opinion and what is fact. Online information has no rules: anyone can say what they like, give their version of history or religion and pretend it is the truth. There should always be someone to say, 'Wait a minute, let's ask some questions, let's listen to a different point of view!'

Some websites supporting ISIS praise the role that young girls and women can have in the jihadi fight, but they deliberately leave out certain aspects that might put people off. What they don't say is that girls can be married from the age of 9 and need permission from males every time they want to go outside the home. Some sites encourage terrorist violence in western countries and give instructions on how to do it. It's difficult to stop these messages because the people who run the sites hide their identity and run the sites from places where no one can prevent them.

Explain that websites supporting jihadist violence have been set up to attract young, lonely or bored people in western countries who are unhappy with their lives and who do not feel they fit into the country or society they are living in. They tell of how Muslims are suffering and being humiliated in other countries. They offer young people a chance to change things by engaging in what they call a war against the enemies of Islam, and describe it as a heroic struggle for a noble cause. Suggest that some of the stories of suffering may be real, and that where there are injustices they should be addressed. But ask the class whether the way to do this is through more violence. Suggest that there are other ways, and discuss alternatives.

Remind pupils of how easy it is to upload a home movie video or to move images around to make people or places look different. How do we know we are being told the truth? Introduce the idea of a puppet master or 'webmaster' who dangles puppets on a string and chooses how to make them move. Suggest that we don't want other people to dangle us on a string like puppets and make us do what they want.

Point out that electronic media can also be used by people who are not terrorists but who want to stir up hatred or violence. Bullying can be done using smartphones and social media. Hate messages may be aimed at individuals or at a particular group of people. The message is that this group of people is a threat. It says that the only way to deal with the threat is to use violence. When there are no rules, it's easy to create an imaginary enemy by making up false reasons. These hate sites focus on a single aspect of identity – like having a black skin or being Jews or Christians or Muslims. The reality is that 'identity' is not one single thing, it has many different forms and aspects, as we will discuss in Unit 5.

OPTIONAL ACTIVITY FOR OLDER PUPILS

Explain that mobile phones have been used in a way that encourages violence.

Give pupils the example of Cronulla, a beachfront suburb of Sydney, in Australia. In December 2005 there were attacks, involving about 5,000 people, between white Australians and Australians whose families had emigrated from the Middle East. Over several days young men on both sides organised violent attacks on each other, causing many injuries and damage to property. The attacks on both sides were organised through text messages. The messages said where the fighting would take place and called on as many people as possible to join in. A reporter on national radio used his breakfast radio programme to repeat   >>

one of the messages that was going around the white Australians. It said people should 'take revenge' by going to Cronulla to beat up their enemies. This was not terrorism; we would call it mob violence or hate crime. But it was very frightening because it showed how quickly violence can spread when hatred is stirred up in an organised way. People who might never use violence on their own feel able to do so when they are in a group. They feel protected by a violent mob or crowd.

Ask pupils for their comments on this. Was the radio reporter who encouraged the violence being responsible? Ask them to think of the difference between violence by one person and violence in a group. They may know of examples in their own experience. (Bullying is sometimes done by groups.) Point out that the opposite can also happen – sometimes we need the support of other people in order to do good things in life – the power of the group can also be positive.

CLASSROOM/ASSEMBLY ACTIVITY

■ Ask the class to imagine a situation such as a case of online bullying or hate messaging affecting a particular (fictitious) individual or a section of the community. How would they deal with this and whom would they involve in the solution?

■ Discuss with pupils what arguments they would use to challenge pro-violence ideas or websites.

> **TIP**
>
> Include amongst the arguments that a one-sided argument was being presented for violence; ask pupils what purpose violence would serve; ask them to think of other ways of helping a suffering population.

4.7 Reporting on terrorism: finding a balance

Remind the class that terrorists want as much attention as possible. They want the media to show film, write and talk about what they do. Remind them that we, the public, want to know what is happening in the world, we don't want to be left in the dark without information. At the same time, we don't want people to get what they want just because they use violence.

Suggest that there are many different ways of reporting terrorism. Each part of the media – newspapers, radio, TV, the Internet and social networking sites – will report it in different ways. Some of what we read or see is by journalists who give both sides of a story. Other people will only ever give one side of the story, their own side. The government will want to make sure that its viewpoint is given. The terrorists will want their views given. And each person doing the reporting wants to be first with the news, and to have a better, more unusual or more exciting story to tell than the others. Telling a story is, after all, what the media are for.

Display a photograph of a high wire artist walking along on a tightrope carrying a long pole to keep his balance. Ask pupils to imagine that he is 'the media'. On one side is 'the government' trying to pull him over to its side; on the other, 'terrorists' are trying to pull him towards them. The tightrope artist has to keep a balance, and be independent of both of them.

Explain to pupils that when a terrorist attack takes place journalists will often turn to members of the government for their views on terrorism. Naturally and correctly, they will report what the government says. But journalists have to be careful because the government may not tell journalists the whole truth; it will just give the government's official side of the story. There may be good reasons for this. The government has a difficult job to do. It must try to keep the population calm and decide what to do next. But a good journalist will not only give the government's views, he or she will look around and see what other sides of the story there might be to tell. There may be facts that are necessary to complete the story.

Most people agree that the media should be free to report a story without interference from the government. If the government puts a **gag** on the media it means they prevent journalists from reporting news that the government wants to keep secret. We call this **censorship**. Suggest that censorship is not a good thing because people have a right to know what is going on. Freedom of the press is an important part of a democracy. During the apartheid period in South Africa journalists could not write freely. There was censorship during the conflict in Bougainville in Papua New Guinea (see Unit 3 case study), and until 2014 there was censorship in Sri Lanka, where journalists who wrote things that the government disapproved of ran the risk of being arrested or beaten up. Nowadays with Internet and social media reporting it's much more difficult for a government to stop people saying or writing what they want.

Remind the class again about how difficult it is for the media to report on terrorism. They are torn between the need to give information about what is going on and the risk of becoming a **mouthpiece** for the views of the terrorists. For this reason, people often have strong opinions on what the media should do about terrorism. Roughly speaking these views divide into three main categories:

(1) *The media, especially TV news, are what keeps terrorism going*; TV is the terrorists' 'oxygen', the terrorists' 'best friend'. Showing terrorist attacks on TV is to give the terrorists exactly what they want. The media should not show terrorism at all, instead they should ignore it.

(2) *The media should show all the horror of what terrorism does to people.* People will be so disgusted at the suffering and violence that they will not support terrorism when they see what it does.

(3) *TV and other media must be free to report on anything that they think is important, including terrorism.* Because of the Internet and social networks, it is impossible for the media to ignore terrorism. Journalists should present the facts as far as possible, and try to give more than one side to the story.

Suggest to the class that there may be times when the media should decide to 'gag' themselves. If journalists have information that would help terrorists, they may choose not to make it public, at least for a while. This might be the case, for example, if police begin to surround a building where terrorists are holding hostages. If journalists talk about this on radio, or if TV cameras show the police moving into position, the terrorists might learn about it and kill the hostages. Sometimes journalists see terrible scenes of killing that are too upsetting to show on television. Most people would agree that they are right not to show them.

You may wish to conclude with the class that the media should be free and that censorship is not a good thing, even if it were possible. You might agree that to decide not to show or not to publish certain things is a good idea occasionally, if to do so would put people's lives at risk, cause more panic or encourage more terrorism. Ideally journalists would choose this 'self-censorship' out of a sense of responsibility.

Remind the class of the attack in Paris in January 2015 on the magazine *Charlie Hebdo* in which 12 people were killed. As the two gunmen left the building they shouted that they had taken revenge for the insult to the Prophet Muhammad, who had been shown in cartoons published by the magazine. The gunmen were tracked down and killed by French special forces two days later.

The magazine had on several occasions published cartoons of the Prophet Muhammad and its staff had received threats because of this. Many Muslims believe that to represent the Prophet in any form is a serious crime under Islamic law. The *Charlie Hebdo* cartoonists had ignored the threats: they continued to draw the Prophet and make fun of Islam, just as they made fun of other religions and published rude cartoons of well-known public figures.

After this attack more than three million people marched in France to defend the freedom of journalists to write and draw what they wanted. People wore badges saying *'Je suis Charlie'* to show their support. Most people think that freedom of expression is an important part of democracy.

The Universal Declaration of Human Rights approved by the United Nations in 1948 states in Article 19:

Everyone has the right to freedom of opinion and expression; this right includes freedom to hold opinions without interference and to seek, receive and impart information and ideas through any media and regardless of frontiers.

In fact, as we know, our freedom of speech is not without limits. We have rights but we also have responsibilities. It is against the law to make a 'hoax' phone call to the police that a bomb is about to explode in a theatre or concert hall when there is no bomb because the resulting panic might put people's lives in danger. There are laws in many countries against 'hate speech' which protect sectors of the population. In school, a pupil who uses bad language or insults a teacher is punished. Most of us accept these limits and probably most of us approve of them. Discuss these examples with the class.

CLASSROOM/ASSEMBLY ACTIVITY

■ Split the class into three groups and hold a debate on the three different viewpoints (pp 88–9) on how the media should report or not on terrorism with each group taking one of the points of view.

■ Discuss the motivations for the *Charlie Hebdo* attacks with the class. In Unit 2, pupils were asked to think about things they most cherished/treasured. Ask them to choose the most important item and imagine that it has been (a) ridiculed, (b) dismissed and (c) misrepresented. How would they feel? What action could be taken to rectify the situation? Ask them to discuss possible ways of resolving this with a friend.

■ Discuss how pupils reacted to hearing about the *Charlie Hebdo* attacks. Some may feel that the journalists were quite right to make fun of whatever they liked, and that no beliefs or individuals should be considered too sacred. Others might say that we can utterly disapprove of the attacks *at the same time as* thinking that the journalists on *Charlie Hebdo* were showing great disrespect for Islam and were wrong to publish them. Just because we condemn the attacks does not necessarily mean we think the cartoons should have been published.

OPTIONAL ACTIVITY FOR OLDER PUPILS

Ask pupils if they think TV news should show everything that a camera captures on film, or whether certain shots (ie of people suffering, injured or dead) should not be shown or whether the media should not give out certain information. Are there things that the public (ie us) should not be told at all?

4.8 Doing deals with terrorists: the media are involved

Return to the idea of a reward. Remind pupils that the terrorists' rewards are the *goals* they want to reach. Terrorists may try to use the media as a tool or instrument to win support for their goals. Remind the class about the Red Brigades in Italy (Unit 3 case study). On one occasion the Red Brigades kidnapped an Italian judge and held him hostage in a secret place. Then they sent a message to all the newspapers. The message explained why the Red Brigades were angry and how they wanted things to change. This message had actually been written by some of the Red Brigades members who were in prison, and it was handed by the prisoners to someone who was allowed to visit them – a family member or a lawyer. It threatened that the Red Brigades would kill the judge in 48 hours unless all the national newspapers printed the message.

Explain that the Italian population – they were the *audience* in this case – were divided over what to do. Some people thought the newspapers should print the message, most people thought not. Most newspapers did not publish the message but one or two did. The judge's family went on TV and his 14-year-old daughter read out part of the terrorists' message. The part she read said that her father was a pig and that he deserved the death sentence. After that the judge was freed.

The terrorists were very happy because they had achieved an important goal: everyone in Italy was discussing them and their message. They were the centre of attention. It didn't really matter whether or not the message was printed in all the papers because just by discussing it, newspapers and TV had given the terrorists all the attention they wanted.

Invite the class to discuss this case, and what they think the right course of action was.

The example above shows how terrorists often try to make a bargain, or do a deal. In the case of the Red Brigades, the bargain was with the media. Explain that sometimes terrorists want to make a bargain with the government. The media are involved in this too, because the media have to explain the point of view of the government, of the terrorists and also of the victims and their families. The way the media reports a story can make a difference to the outcome. This might happen, for example, if terrorists are holding hostages and threatening to kill them unless the government frees terrorist prisoners. The media will report all the human stories of the families and this will put the government under great pressure.

> **TIP**
> The optional information for older pupils is based on a real life case from the Netherlands. If you think that it might cause alarm then pass directly to the summary.

OPTIONAL INFORMATION FOR OLDER PUPILS

In 1977 terrorists took 105 children and five teachers hostage in a primary school in the Dutch town of Bovensmilde. The terrorists wanted members of their group to be released from prison. The children were shut in two classrooms and told by the terrorists to cover the windows with newspaper so no one could see in. Food and water were sent into the school from outside. After four days many of the children had stomach upsets, and eventually the terrorists allowed them all to leave the school, a few at a time. Four teachers were kept as hostages. More than two weeks later Dutch soldiers raided the school. The terrorist group gave up without a fight and no one was hurt. No prisoners were allowed out of prison. There was great media interest in the story, especially when so many children were hostages, and this put particular pressure on the government to make a bargain with the terrorists.

Explain that the government is in a very difficult position when terrorists make their demands. The government can refuse to make any kind of bargain. If a government refuses to negotiate it may order the police or army to use force to capture the terrorists. But there is a risk that the terrorists will start killing the hostages. The government may send a very skilled person to talk to the terrorists. That person is called a **negotiator**. He or she will talk to the terrorists as well as the government, and try to find a way out of the crisis.

Invite the class to discuss the choice between doing what terrorists want and people being hurt. Explain that the problem about making bargains is that it may save lives on one occasion, but it may lead to more violence if terrorists are released from prison or if terrorists think they can try the same tactic again.

SUMMARY UNIT 4

Remind pupils of what they have learned in this Unit:

■ The media give us the means of *information, communication* and *sharing*.

■ Journalists have responsibilities to tell the truth as far as possible and report facts.

■ Terrorists need the media to show what they have done and to communicate their *message*.

■ Terrorism is a *performance* involving *victims*, a *target* and an *audience*.

■ Terrorists attack a *symbol* of what they are angry about.　　>>

- Terrorists want to *change people's behaviour*. The behaviour they most want to change is that of the target, usually a government or other authority. But they also want to change what ordinary people do.

- The media can influence public opinion in ways that help to understand and resolve conflict. They can also be used to encourage hatred and violence.

- We need to have ways of checking our sources of information because websites can give us misleading or false stories.

- Censorship of terrorist activities is impossible nowadays in most countries, even if it were a good thing. Most people agree that the media should be free but responsible.

- Doing a deal with terrorists is a risky thing to do and can lead to more terrorism.

Conclude with the class that when it comes to reporting on terrorism the media have a very difficult and responsible job to carry out.

CLASSROOM/ASSEMBLY ACTIVITY

- Ask the class to make a list of the most important tasks for a journalist. Help them towards answers such as: presenting different sides of a story; choosing words very carefully; being careful to separate facts from opinions.

- Ask the class to present a TV news story about a robbery at an imaginary shop near the school. Ask them to write down (a) the facts they need to know and (b) the important people to interview who can help to tell the story (the shop-owner, the people who live upstairs, someone who was driving past at the time of the robbery, the local police who are investigating, etc). Split them into groups, each group representing a different side of the story. Ask them to present the event as a news item, with the important individuals being interviewed and each giving their story. A 'newsreader' introduces the story and 'goes live' to journalists who ask the questions. This can be performed in an assembly as a class drama.

- Alternatively, invite them to present the Bowmarket story and kidnap from Unit 1 in this way.

- Ask pupils how they can judge online information sources.

Unit 5:
Pulling It All Together

KEY VOCABULARY

truce: a stop or halt to fighting (usually lasting longer than a cease-fire)

betray: to deceive, to be disloyal to, to help the enemies of

mediator: someone who helps people to talk to each other when they disagree strongly about something

dominate: to lead or be the strongest member of a group

reconciliation: a way of making peace, bringing people back together

tradition: a custom or belief that is passed down through generations

dialect: a local or regional form of a main language

court: a place where legal cases are heard and decisions about justice are made; also a group of people who make legal decisions in a courtroom, for example a judge and jury

offender: someone who commits an offence or crime

fine: a sum of money that is paid as a punishment for breaking the law

prison sentence: a fixed time that someone must spend in prison after breaking the law

restorative justice: justice that repairs the harm that has been done after a crime has been committed

Remembrance Day: a day when people remember those who have died as a result of war or conflict

amputate: cut off

campaign: to work for a cause, or to work to make something happen

Ubuntu: (from the Nguni group of African languages) a sense of belonging together, caring for one another

beacon: signal or sign that helps people to find their way

Aim and content of Unit 5

The first part of Unit 5 introduces some of the factors that contribute to the cessation of terrorism and shows how the wounds that remain can be healed once conflict is over. Various approaches to reconciliation are explained and the importance of Courageous People is stressed, both in the context of overcoming terrorism and in other spheres. Pupils are reminded that each person's identity has many different aspects, and that our 'multiple identities' help us to find the common ground and interests that are part of our shared citizenship. The Unit shows how diversity is positive and contributes greatly to our lives. The importance of dialogue and mutual respect is emphasised, and pupils are encouraged to practise these in their own lives.

The second part of Unit 5 helps pupils to recall what they have learned from the previous units of the book as a lead into conclusions. A definition of terrorism is proposed. It is suggested that terrorism may never go away completely, but that, as it is people who are responsible for terrorism, it is also people who can make it go away.

The questionnaire is repeated at the end of the Unit.

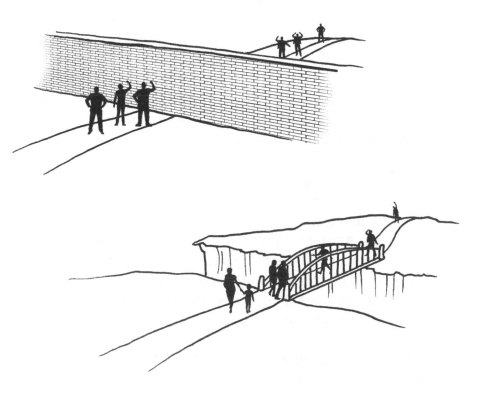

We should build bridges not walls between people

Radicalisation and Terrorism: A Teacher's Handbook for Addressing Extremism

LEARNING OUTCOMES

By the end of Unit 5, pupils will be able to:

- explain how conflicts end, and identify some of the factors that lead to this
- use classroom situations and their own experiences to explore how peaceful relations between people can be restored, emphasising the importance of dialogue, 'respectful listening' and the value of diversity within shared citizenship
- examine the contribution made by peacemakers, here called 'Courageous People', to solving conflict and overcoming hatred
- challenge ideas of hatred and revenge by acknowledging past injustices and by looking for common ground for peace
- participate in a debate on the definition of terrorism, using terms explored in previous Units
- draw conclusions from the experiences of reconciliation in South Africa and the peace process in Northern Ireland

RECOMMENDED MATERIALS

Paper and drawing materials

Class photocopies of:
- the questionnaire (PCM1)
- Ruskin Bond's poem 'If mice could roar' (PCM5)
- Cover of this Handbook

Photo images of:
- Dr Desmond Tutu (ideally one with Nelson Mandela)

Notes for teachers

Unit 5.6 should be covered to the extent that you have time to recap on the whole Handbook. If (after completing 5.1– 5.5) you have insufficient time or if you have covered the different issues to your satisfaction, proceed directly to the conclusions in 5.7 and 5.8.

At the end of the Unit we return to the problem of finding a universal definition of terrorism. More appropriate to older classes, this encourages pupils to find a working definition based on what has been studied to date. Before you begin, we recommend you re-read the section *Definitions, Terminology and Sources* and remind yourself of the 14 UN Conventions regarding terrorist acts discussed in Unit 3.4, listed in endnote 31.

5.1 Does terrorism ever go away, and how?

Explain to the class that terrorism can and does go away. This can happen for many different reasons, including the following:

Terrorists win their battle

This happens rarely, but it's not impossible. If terrorists have a lot of support from people in their own or in other countries for their struggle, then they may win. For this reason the terrorists stop being terrorists, and they become the new government. Terrorism stops because the terrorists have been successful in achieving their goals.

The terrorists and the government agree on a peace plan

This may happen when either the terrorist group, or the government, or both, realise that they can never win outright victory. To begin with, all they agree on is to hold secret talks. (Governments often say that

> *Let's move on from terrorism*

they do not talk to terrorists – though they often do – because they don't want the media to report it.) While the talks are going on the terrorists may call a **truce**: this is like a cease-fire, but one that lasts long enough to discuss possibilities for peace. The government will also make a promise, perhaps to allow more family visits to terrorists in prison, or to move prisoners to a jail nearer their home. If things go well, terrorists and government reach an agreement. It will probably be a compromise, which means neither side gets everything it wants, but there is enough common ground to call a halt to violence. Eventually the terrorists may agree to give up their weapons, or leave them in a place where they cannot touch them. People who do not belong to the government or to the terrorist group will make sure that this happens. This took place in Northern Ireland and in Bougainville, Papua New Guinea.

Terrorism may stop when special laws are passed

These laws may increase punishments for terrorists and anyone who helps them. If most leaders and members of the group are arrested, either no one is left to carry on, or people are too frightened to do so. Governments must be careful about this, however. They must be careful not to *overreact*, that is, to respond too strongly. Most citizens are not terrorists and if laws against terrorism are too strict they make everyone less free. For example if a government reacts to terrorism by passing a new law that allows people to be kept in prison without trial for a long time then the human rights of the whole population suffer. There is a much better chance of terrorism going away if a country has fair laws and gives everyone, terrorists included, a fair trial. New laws can help to end terrorism if they encourage people to abandon terrorist groups and give up violence. Sometimes a law is introduced that encourages terrorists to 'tell tales' on one another. That means if a terrorist helps police to arrest other terrorists, he/she may not have to go to prison at all, or will be freed after a short time. Terrorists who do this run the risk of being killed by former companions, so they need help to move to a country where no one knows them, and to live a new life under a different name. This kind of law has been used in Northern Ireland and in Italy.

Terrorism ends because of quarrels inside the group

Terrorists disagree among themselves about their goals or their methods. Sometimes they quarrel about personal matters. If they start to fight each other it is more likely that members will leave the group or that someone will **betray** them to the police and the remaining members will be arrested.

The terrorist group loses support among the population that has supported it

This can happen for many reasons. The terrorist violence may have gone too far and the methods seem wrong, even to the people who share the same goals. If this happens we can say that the sea in which the terrorist fish have been swimming has dried up. The supporters or members of a terrorist group may become weary of violence; they decide that it is destructive for everyone. They realise that violence is not bringing them any closer to their goals. Governments or other authorities may also realise this, and can set a peace plan in motion. This doesn't always mean that governments start talking to terrorists. They may start talking to people who share the terrorists' goals and who are in touch with the terrorist leaders. If a government does this then it learns what the real problems are, and why the protests have been so angry and violent. The government may be able to change things and make things better without having to talk to terrorists or making an actual bargain with them. Ideally, this should happen before terrorism even starts.

The government and the terrorist group ask for outside help

They may decide that they need help from **mediators** to be able to talk to each other. A mediator is like a referee in a football game – someone who is completely outside the conflict and has no *bias* in favour of one side or the other. Mediators can sometimes help because they are calm when members of the two sides are angry and feel like shouting at one other. When many people have been murdered on both sides, emotions may be too strong for them to have a calm dialogue. For several years the Norwegian government acted as mediator in peace talks between the government of Sri Lanka and the Liberation Tigers of Tamil Eelam who wanted an independent homeland in Sri Lanka for the Tamil people. In Bougainville the New Zealand government acted as a mediator between the rebels and the government of Papua New Guinea (see Unit 3).

CLASSROOM/ASSEMBLY ACTIVITY

- ■ Invite the class to give their views on the above. Split pupils into groups and ask them to imagine an argument that takes place over something in their own lives at home or school. Examples could include:
  - ● a young girl is going to a party and wants to wear something which is very fashionable at the moment. Her mother doesn't think that it is suitable and tells her that she can't go to the party unless she finds something different to wear. Both sides will not move
  - ● at home, a family of four children is arguing about which programme to watch on the only TV in the house. The two oldest children want to watch something that the younger children would not understand

>>

- every day the same group of children play football, but the teams always have the same people in them. This causes hurt and upset to other children who never have the opportunity to play
- pupils in a school class are working on a presentation as a group. Two of the pupils **dominate** and do all the talking. Their opinions are the only ones to be heard. How can the other pupils have their voices heard?

Ask the class to work out how the problems can be resolved, using other members of the class or adults as mediators if appropriate.

5.2 Healing the wounds

Invite the class to think about the suffering that terrorism and conflict bring to a country. Children are left without parents, parents are left without sons or daughters, whole families have suffered in ways that cause nightmares for a long time to come.

Explain that even when conflict ends, it does not mean an end of suffering for the populations involved. For those who have lost a loved one the loss may be felt more strongly when life returns to normal for everyone else. Many people will still have feelings of anger and even hatred for the other side, though they are relieved that the conflict has ended. Help pupils to understand this with the idea of a deep leg wound. The wound heals but a scar remains and the leg still hurts. Occasionally the leg bangs against something; the wound opens again and starts to bleed.

Explain that South Africa has led the way in its efforts to bring people back together after conflict. We call this **reconciliation**. It means overcoming differences and helping people to live in peace with one another. President Nelson Mandela set up a special meeting place where people and families who had suffered violence and torture were invited to tell their stories. Those who had carried out the violence were invited to confess their crimes. This was called the Truth and Reconciliation Commission. The Chairman of the Commission was Dr Desmond Tutu, the former Archbishop of Cape Town, who had won the Nobel Peace Prize in 1984 for his commitment to non-violent protest against apartheid. Some 20,000 individual accounts of suffering were given in evidence. Around 7,000 people who had committed violence came to the Commission to tell their stories in public, often for the first time. The sessions were open to the public and shown on TV. When those who had carried out the violence told the whole truth about what they had done, they could ask to be forgiven.

Explain that in countries such as Liberia, Uganda, Rwanda and Sierra Leone civil wars lasted for years. Thousands of children were taken from their families and forced to become part of a fighting group. These young soldiers saw terrible violence and had terrible violence done to them. They needed special help, both to overcome this and to enable them to learn all the things that they had missed by not going to school.

Tell pupils about 'Project Hope' that began in Gulu district, Northern Uganda in 2007. During the 20 years of civil war in Uganda about 20,000 children were kidnapped and forced to join a terrorist group called the Lord's Resistance Army. Project Hope was set up by the government of Uganda, with support from the Commonwealth Secretariat. Its aim was to help some 200 former child soldiers to learn new skills and to live in a peaceful way. The project had several parts: one offered the chance for young people to go back to school and have the education that they missed. Another part gave them the chance to talk through their terrible experiences with people who were specially trained to help them, and who taught them how they could live in a peaceful way. A third group of trainers helped them to develop skills in farming, metalwork, carpentry, tree planting and other useful occupations. The aim was to help them find a job and prevent them returning to violence.[37]

CLASSROOM/ASSEMBLY ACTIVITY

- Invite the class to think of ways in which storytelling can help people to deal with grief and loss. Suggest that loss may be more bearable when it is shared, when other people say, 'Yes, I know that feeling too.' Examples could include: joining a group of people, each of whom has lost someone dear to them and talking through the experience; talking to a close friend/ relative/teacher about a special day shared with a grandparent or parent who has died; trying to get over the loss of a beloved pet by remembering the naughty or funny things it used to do.

- Discuss the different kinds of help provided by Project Hope. Ask children which they think is the most important aspect of it, and why.

- Discuss (with older pupils) whether a programme of this kind, suitably adapted, could/should be introduced with young western fighters returning to Europe from Syria/Iraq. What differences would there be? Who should be involved?

5.3 We are all the colours of the rainbow

Remind the class that South Africa is often called 'the rainbow nation' because of the many different races who live there and all the languages that are spoken. All its citizens belong to the same country – South Africa – but in it there are many different identities, **traditions** and faiths.

Point out that India is also a country of multiple identities: Indians have an identity as members of a caste, a religion and a community as well as being speakers of one or more languages. In addition to Hindi and English – the two official languages – 22 regional languages are recognised by the Indian Constitution and each of them has hundreds of different **dialects**.

Suggest that we all have different identities for the different parts of our lives, for example at school, in the family, or through some aspect of our community life. Ask pupils to think of their mother or of another woman who is close to them. That same woman can be a mother, a daughter and a sister, as well as being a teacher or a doctor or a shopkeeper. In the course of each day the different parts of her identity cause her to do different activities, play a different role and speak in a different way. Her identity is a mix of all these things together, even if one or other role is more important at certain moments of the day.

Go back to the idea of a rainbow nation.

Ask the class what the most beautiful thing about a rainbow is. Suggest that the rainbow is beautiful because all the colours are there, each of them different. Would pupils always want to wear only one colour of clothes every day? Do they think that every flower, fruit and vegetable should be the same colour? We like the world to be different and varied. Suggest that we want people to be different too. Diversity, or differences, should not be a reason to fear or hate (as was discussed in Unit 4). And it doesn't prevent us from sharing things like an interest in keeping a pet, in a particular kind of music or sport, in flying saucers or Sudoku. We are all citizens of a community such as a school, but also of a wider local community where we live or worship, play sport or make music. Sharing citizenship with others means our interests and our identities are always overlapping and connecting with each other. We are not fixed in a single photo frame of identity, we move and change and cross over.

CLASSROOM/ASSEMBLY ACTIVITY

- Discuss language and dialect with the class, and ask them to think of examples of differences between the dialect in your area and the country's official language.

- Ask pupils to think of the differences between their lives and those of children in a different part of the same country (eg city/rural communities or north/south).

- Ask every pupil who has a sister to stand up. This is a group of people that have something in common. Do the same exercise with: every pupil who can say something in more than one language; every pupil who has a relative in another country; who has a cat or a dog; or who has experienced the death of a family member. Discuss how membership of each group overlaps with others. Point out how each group shares something, but how that something is also what makes the group different from another one. Suggest all these identities are important and help to make us who we are. They can be used to find *common ground* with other people. Remind them of the saying, 'We all smile in the same language.'

- Alternatively do the same exercise using a diagram. Ask pupils to draw an outline of themselves. Inside it they should write all the different aspects of their lives. They should show where and how their lives overlap with others.

- Ask the class to imagine or to draw a bridge, with people going back and forward, meeting and talking to each other. Then ask them to imagine or draw a high wall between two groups of people. A bridge allows us to communicate and share; the wall puts up a barrier. We are more likely to fear people when we cannot see or talk to them.

5.4 Reconciliation and restoring justice – old traditions can help

Discuss with the class how they learn to express their views inside the classroom. Remind them how they use(d) circle time: pupils sit in a circle and take it in turns to give an opinion. Sometimes an object is passed round from pupil to pupil. Whoever has the object – a book, a stick or a piece of cloth – has the right to speak and everyone else must listen.

Ask pupils if they have heard of circle courts or circle remedies. This is a kind of **court**, usually in a small community, which brings together an **offender** – someone who has committed a crime – with the *victim* of the crime. The families and other members of the community are also involved. This kind of justice belongs to a very old tradition for Aboriginal communities in Canada and Australia and in many of the Pacific Islands. It is different to the justice that we see in most courtrooms.

Explain the difference: usually, when a crime is committed by an adult, the offender is punished with a **fine** or a **prison sentence**. The victims are left to cope with the effects of the crime as best they can. With circle courts, everyone sits down together; they discuss the harm that has been done, what the *consequences* have been for everyone involved, and decide together how to make things better. There is usually someone who leads the discussion and who asks the questions. This can often lead to reconciliation. The victim may forgive the offender, and the offender, who has accepted his or her responsibility, will probably not commit the offence again.

Explain that this kind of justice is called **restorative justice** because it puts back or restores relationships between members of a community. It makes an individual face up to the harm that has been done, accept that it has had bad consequences, and restores respect between people. These methods were used in Bougainville, Papua New Guinea after the conflict there. They have also been used to deal with violent behaviour in primary and secondary schools, especially in Canada, Australia and New Zealand. For example, if one pupil has bullied another, both pupils will talk about the behaviour, why it happened and its consequences. The behaviour is bad, and everyone can agree on this, but the boy or girl is not necessarily a bad person. The label 'bad' belongs to the behaviour, not to the person. If we put the label of 'bully' on someone then there is a risk of him/her being stuck with that one identity only. He/she can't change or move on and nor can the victim.

Explain that when we use restorative justice, everyone who has been affected by the violent behaviour has a voice and a share in what happens. Behaviour can change and everyone can move on. In one school a 'detention room' was turned into a 'conference room'. That is, a room for punishment became a room where things were discussed. It involves 'respectful listening' because everyone has a chance to tell his or her story and be listened to by others. It's not so different to what happened in South Africa.

CLASSROOM/ASSEMBLY ACTIVITY

■ Ask pupils to think of objects at home and in school that can be easily broken. Can they all be fixed? Ask them to sort them into a 'can-be-fixed' group and a 'can't-be-fixed' group. If a pupil breaks something valuable that belongs to someone else, he/she can help to mend it again.

■ If appropriate, lead on sensitively to the idea of broken relationships. These can break down too, and walls are put up.

■ Ask pupils to devise a scenario where harm has been done to some pupils in the school by others, or else where children have done some harm to members of the community.

■ Ask pupils to return to the Bowmarket Storyline in Unit 1. Ask them to imagine that Ben, John and Amy had not been sent to prison but had discussed their behaviour and its consequences with Rachel Brown's family and the Bowmarket community. Ask them to set up a 'respectful listening conference', where each person plays a part and has a voice. How could Ben, John and Amy be reconciled with the Brown family and the Bowmarket community?

> **TIP**
>
> An example: some children sold fake raffle tickets to senior citizens. After a conference was held the children paid back the money and did gardening work for some of the people they had wronged.

5.5 Courageous People

Explain that special individuals sometimes play an important role in helping violence to end, or in helping a community to live together in a more peaceful way. We can call them 'Courageous People'.

Point out that many of them have known terrible loss or suffering themselves. A shopkeeper called Gordon Wilson from Northern Ireland was standing beside his young daughter at a **Remembrance Day** ceremony in the town of Enniskillen in 1987 when an IRA bomb exploded, killing her and ten others. Once he recovered from his injuries he decided to spend the rest of his life in efforts to bring peace to Northern Ireland. He had suffered so much that he wanted to stop other people from going through the same pain.

In other cases, prime ministers, presidents or other important politicians take a great risk by starting peace talks with terrorists. If it all goes wrong and more people are killed then the politicians may become very unpopular and no one will vote for them. They also put their own lives at risk. Premier Theodore Miriung of Bougainville, Papua New Guinea, was a Courageous Person who tried to bring about peace but was murdered. (See Unit 3.6)

Explain that Dr Desmond Tutu and former president Nelson Mandela can both be described as Courageous People. Nelson Mandela spent 27 years in prison but said he didn't hate the white rulers of his country who put him there. He said he wanted peace, not revenge. When he came out of prison he shook hands with his jailers and started working towards a peaceful end to conflict in South Africa. After so many years of violence and hatred, it was amazing that South Africa could change to democracy in a peaceful way. Dr Tutu said that all South Africans had been wounded by the terrible things that had happened in their country. But he said they were 'wounded healers', that they were able to help other people precisely because they had suffered so much.

Tell the class about another Courageous Person (but in a different way), a New Zealander called Percy Murphy from Whenuapai, near Auckland. Percy was the son of a poor Irish father and a Maori mother. He suffered discrimination at the white school he attended because of his mixed race and because the Maori language and culture were not respected. During World War 2 he joined the Maori battalion of the New Zealand army and at 18 he was sent thousands of miles away to fight in Europe. The Maori soldiers in his company often frightened the enemy by performing their Haka war dance, something we still see today at New Zealand rugby team matches. In 1943, during a fierce battle in Italy, Percy Murphy stepped on a landmine and later his right leg had to be **amputated**. When he returned to New Zealand, Percy continued to fight but in a different way. First he worked to improve the rights of Maori soldiers who had fought for their country. He became one of New Zealand's first Maori mayors in Murupara, on North Island. Remembering his unhappy childhood, he then **campaigned** for the right of Maori people to be educated about their own culture and in the Maori language, *te reo*. His efforts led to the setting up of pre-school 'language nests' or *kōhanga reo*, for Maori children. Thanks to him every teacher in New Zealand has to study and give classes in Maori culture; every university has a *marae* or sacred meeting place where Maori students can take part in their cultural and spiritual traditions.[38] (Percy Murphy died in 2009 at the age of 85.)

CLASSROOM/ASSEMBLY ACTIVITY

- Invite children to reflect on the examples given. Ask them what qualities are necessary for a Courageous Person (apart from courage!).

- Invite them to think of someone who has made a special contribution to the well-being of their own community. What was special about him/her?

5.6 Optional revision discussions

If you have time, take the opportunity to recap on what's been learned to this point.

What is and isn't terrorism? (Unit 1)

Remind pupils of where we started on our journey through the subject of terrorism.

We began with the idea of a cooking pot, into which we put various ingredients for terrorism. Ask pupils to recall the main ingredients:

- the use or threat of violence to cause terror, usually by non-state individuals or groups, ie not acting for a state or government
- grievances (strong feelings of anger, disappointment and hatred) that are blamed on an enemy and the desire to take revenge
- the use of violence against 'ordinary people' or civilians
- goals of political power that are not just for one person but for a community
- the belief that violence is the only way to reach the goals
- the aim of attracting as much attention, or publicity, as possible
- the aim of sending a message to change the behaviour of an authority or the people in charge

Ask pupils what they remember about Mahatma Gandhi and Martin Luther King. What were their views about protest? Ask them who Rosa Parks was, and why she was important.

Is terrorism new or old? (Unit 2)

Ask pupils what they remember about the Assassins and the Thugs.

What were the goals of the Suffragettes? What methods did they use? Were women given the vote because (a) they used violence or (b) they helped in the war effort or (c) both?

Remind pupils about two periods where peaceful protest was difficult, if not impossible: France during World War 2 and South Africa during apartheid. Ask them why it was so difficult to protest peacefully.

Was Nelson Mandela a terrorist or a man of peace? Why? What is the meaning of a *just cause*?

How do we know that people change their minds about what a just cause is? (Answer: Few people would say nowadays that black and coloured South Africans should not have the same rights as white South Africans, or that women should not be allowed to vote. Plenty of people said so in the past.)

The jigsaw of terrorism (Unit 3)

Ask pupils to tell the story of Bobo and his family in their own words. Try to establish the most important elements of the story: ie Grandfather's storytelling; Sam being humiliated and taking revenge; Bobo meeting the two women; Bobo's feelings of not belonging, and the need to 'do something'; Bobo's return to Exland and what he discovered about violence.

Remind pupils that terrorism is a bit like a jigsaw puzzle. What are the sections we need to begin to piece together the puzzle (ie to understand terrorism)? We need to know:

- the *reasons* why people become terrorists (Why are they angry and why do they think things are unfair?)
- the *goals* or rewards that terrorists want to achieve (What do they want?)
- the *methods*, or the things that terrorists do, and to whom (How do terrorists use violence?)
- the influences and experiences that may lead an individual to choose violence (What are the *pathways* into terrorism?)

Remind pupils that it is useful to separate the reasons, goals and methods of terrorism. Why is this important? Suggest that we can sometimes agree with the reasons for – and perhaps the goals of – terrorism but this does not mean we agree with the methods.

The case studies

Ask pupils to say in their own words what they remember about terrorism in Northern Ireland. What were the goals of the different sides?

Why were the Red Brigades angry and what did they hate about Italy? What was their goal? What happens when there is a revolution?

What are the goals of Al-Qaeda and ISIS? Who is the enemy for these groups, and why?

Ask pupils to tell the story of the conflict in Bougainville, Papua New Guinea. Why were the people of Bougainville angry? What had happened there? How did the government react to the protest? Who were the important people that helped to bring peace in Bougainville? (Eg Courageous People, women's groups, the New Zealand government)

Walking the tightrope – terrorism and the media (Unit 4)

Invite pupils to remember how the media provides us with news and information.

Ask them to describe the differences between the *victims*, the *target* and the *audience* of terrorism.

Invite them to say how the media become involved with the terrorists' *message*.

Ask the class to say what responsibilities journalists have when they report on terrorism. Why does it matter what they write, and how they write it? What are the risks that they run?

Ask the class how terrorism, the Internet and social media are connected. *(They can be used to encourage people to join a group that supports or uses violence. They can also be used to communicate positive messages that help to prevent conflict.)*

Discuss what *censorship* is and whether it is ever a good thing. Remind pupils of the principle of freedom of expression. Should journalists or other people always be free to say or write what they want?

Ask the class what the possible risks and the possible benefits are of making bargains with terrorists.

You may choose here either to discuss a definition of terrorism or to pass directly to *5.8 Final thoughts on terrorism*.

5.7 The problem of 'defining' terrorism

Remind pupils that whenever we use the word terrorism we are telling other people that we disapprove of it. Terrorism comes with the label saying 'wrong behaviour' on it. Yet no one can quite agree on exactly what it is that makes it wrong. Remind them of the saying 'One man's terrorist is another man's freedom fighter' that was discussed in Unit 3.3. Invite them to say why this is an unhelpful way of looking at terrorism: *because it depends on opinion, not fact*. It depends on whether someone agrees with the goals or not.

We tried to overcome this problem by looking at terrorist *methods*. If we looked at methods then we were talking about facts, not opinions. Many international agreements or Conventions have been made on this basis, like the 14 UN Conventions on terrorism, discussed in 3.4. The Conventions state that certain kinds of behaviour must be considered as crimes, and that they must be punished wherever they occur. They refer to attacks on *public buildings*, on *public transport* or

> *Let's draw some conclusions*

on *public services* like energy or water supplies. There is agreement about these attacks because they involve the use or threat of violence to *civilians*: ordinary men, women and children going about their daily lives. The Conventions also include attacks on diplomats: people who represent their country or an international organisation abroad.

Having reminded yourself of the explanations given in *Definitions, Terminology and Sources*, invite pupils now to suggest their own definition of terrorism and/or suggest the following definition. Say that it will probably not satisfy everyone, but it draws on the ingredients of terrorism that we have explored in this Handbook. In particular, it overcomes our main problem: it looks at *methods* of terrorism and does not depend on opinion or bias.

> *Terrorism is deliberate violence or the threat of violence for political goals, usually by non-state individuals or groups, against a civilian population. It is used to cause terror and to send a message to a wider audience, and aims to force a section of the population, an authority or a government to change its behaviour.*

Discuss each element of this proposed definition in turn, and invite the class to contribute their thoughts. Be open to alternative suggestions.

5.8 Final thoughts on terrorism

Conclude with the class that terrorism can and usually does go away, though it may take a long time. We have seen this for ourselves with the examples in this Handbook.

Ask them what is needed for terrorism to end. Encourage answers such as:

● people must be fed up with violence and want to live in peace
● we need Courageous People who are ready to stand up for peace
● laws should be fair to all groups in a population
● we should be ready to ask for help from mediators
● we should build bridges not walls between people
● we must try to go beyond feelings of hatred and the desire for revenge

Suggest that terrorism will probably never disappear completely. Somewhere in the world there will always be people who have feelings of hatred and anger for an enemy, people who have grievances and who feel that taking violence into their own hands is the only way to achieve their goals.

But (ask the class) if we look back at history and around the world, do we see anything good that ever comes from terrorism? Suggest that the answer is 'No' and terrorism is always destructive. Former terrorists have said, many years later, that it brought as much harm to their own community as to the other side.[39]

Suggest that most people do not want to live with war and conflict going on around them. Most people do not want hatred to pass down from generation to generation. They would prefer to live in peace with other human beings, to work and go to school and enjoy leisure time with friends. Terrorism *can and does* come to an end. It means putting anger and hatred to one side, even if we cannot forget them. It means accepting that disagreements will always divide people, but trying to build bridges across them. It means looking for common ground where one day trust may grow.

Make the following point very clear to the class: *making peace doesn't mean that enemies have to become friends*.

As Lord Alderdice, who helped to bring about the peace agreement in Northern Ireland, has said:

> *How can we feel respect for people who we believe have wronged us and done terrible things? In truth we cannot feel respect, but we can behave with respect … It is not about agreeing with your opponents, rather it is about how to disagree without resorting to abusing and killing each other.*[40]

Former enemies can learn to talk to each other with respect. They can look for what unites them rather than what divides them. They can make and keep promises and respect agreements that have been made. If possible, someone outside the conflict should be there to see that this happens. Then peace will have a chance.

Dr Desmond Tutu often talks about the importance of the word **Ubuntu** in the Nguni group of African languages. When people have *Ubuntu* it means they are generous, friendly and caring people, whose lives are closely tied up with other people's lives. He reminds us of the African saying, 'A person is a person through other people.' It means that everyone belongs to and depends on everyone else around them. Nelson Mandela believed this too. He told the white rulers of South Africa that *they* would only be free when *all* South Africans were free.

Remind pupils (recalling Unit 1) that just as people are responsible for terrorism, people can make it go away. Terrorism will not go away as long as people look for revenge rather than peace.

At the end of his work as Chairman of the Truth and Reconciliation Commission, Dr Tutu said this:

> *When we look around us at some of the conflict areas of the world, it becomes clear that there is not much of a future for them without forgiveness, without reconciliation. God has blessed us richly so that we might be a blessing to others. Quite improbably, we as South Africans have become a* **beacon** *of hope to others locked in deadly conflict that peace, that a just resolution, is possible. If it could happen in South Africa then it can certainly happen anywhere else.*[41]

Suggest that without Courageous People like Dr Tutu and Nelson Mandela, South Africa might still be a country in conflict.

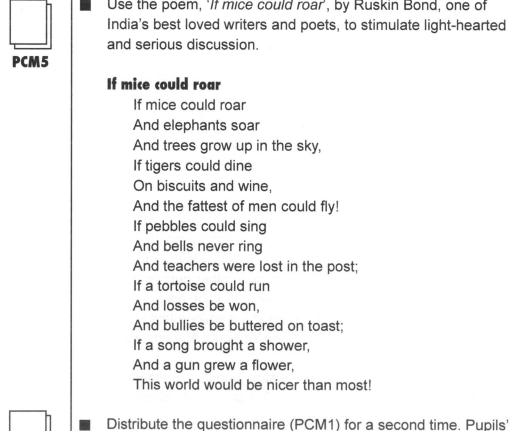

CLASSROOM/ASSEMBLY ACTIVITY

■ Ask the class to 'stand up for' or 'shout out for' things that they want to happen.

■ Ask them to suggest ideas or projects that would make the world a better place.

■ Use the poem, '*If mice could roar*', by Ruskin Bond, one of India's best loved writers and poets, to stimulate light-hearted and serious discussion.

PCM5

If mice could roar

If mice could roar
And elephants soar
And trees grow up in the sky,
If tigers could dine
On biscuits and wine,
And the fattest of men could fly!
If pebbles could sing
And bells never ring
And teachers were lost in the post;
If a tortoise could run
And losses be won,
And bullies be buttered on toast;
If a song brought a shower,
And a gun grew a flower,
This world would be nicer than most!

■ Distribute the questionnaire (PCM1) for a second time. Pupils' answers should differ considerably from those given at the start of study.

PCM1

OPTIONAL ACTIVITY FOR OLDER PUPILS

■ Make photocopies of the cover of this Handbook. Invite the class to explore what is happening in each photo.

■ *Top left*: The Twin Towers of the World Trade Center, New York, shortly after two hijacked planes had been crashed into the Towers. Remind pupils that the Twin Towers were a symbol of American power and wealth. (Unit 4 p 82) Cameras filmed the second plane hitting the South Tower and the whole world could watch on TV as the Towers collapsed. Invite pupils to think about how the mass media should deal with terrorism and what the problems are.

■ *Top right*: South African President Nelson Mandela with Dr Desmond Tutu, Chair of the Truth and Reconciliation Commission in Pretoria, 29 October 1998. On this day the Commission presented President Mandela with the results of its 2½ year investigation into the terrible injustices and violence done during the apartheid years from 1960–1994. Five large volumes were presented on this day. (Two more volumes completed in 2003 examined how the Commission itself had worked). Discuss the notion of 'wounded healers' (Unit 5 p 104) with the class and how/if they think the pain and suffering of conflict can ever be healed.

■ *Middle left*: School children in Mumbai preparing to take part in a march for peace on 20 July 2011. One week earlier three terrorist bomb attacks in the city had killed 26 people and injured 130 more. Remind children of the UN Convention on the Rights of the Child which says that children have rights that include the right to grow up in peace, to go to school and to have health care. Ask the class to think of people who are important peacemakers. Answer: women (Bougainville case study Unit 3.6 p 71) and Courageous People (Unit 5.5 p 103).

■ *Middle right*: Two survivors of the London transport bombings of 7 July 2005. When the bombs exploded in the London Underground complete strangers helped each other out of the tunnels. Sometimes great friendship can come out of the most terrible events. Discuss with the class how sharing grief and sadness with people who have had the same experience can make things better. (Unit 5.2 p 99)

>>

■ **Bottom left**: A child soldier wearing a teddy bear backpack in Liberia, West Africa in 2003. Invite the class to say why this is strange: ie that he is just a child and has a childish pink rucksack, but at the same time he is a soldier and is pointing a gun at the photographer. Ask them to imagine what that moment must have been like for the photographer. Discuss the life of child soldiers and how they can go back to normal life. (Unit 5.2 p 99)

■ **Bottom right**: Pupils in a classroom. Invite the class to give their views on the course of study in this Handbook, and what they particularly liked or did not like about the lessons.

Questionnaire

1. When you hear the word 'terrorism', what other words come into your mind?

2. How do you think people become terrorists?

3. Why do you think terrorists kill and injure people?

4. If you could talk to a terrorist what would you say?

5. How do you think we could make terrorism go away?

Dreams

Extract from Dr Martin Luther King Jr's 'I have a dream' speech (28 August, 1963)

'Let us not seek to satisfy our thirst for freedom by drinking from the cup of bitterness and hatred. We must forever conduct our struggle on the high plane of dignity and discipline. We must not allow our creative protest to degenerate into physical violence. Again and again, we must rise to the majestic heights of meeting physical force with soul force …

'I have a dream that one day on the red hills of Georgia, the sons of former slaves and the sons of former slave owners will be able to sit down together at the table of brotherhood … I have a dream that my four little children will one day live in a nation where they will not be judged by the color of their skin but by the content of their character.'

• •

Let no one steal your dreams

Let no one steal your dreams
Let no one tear apart
The burning of ambition
That fires the drive inside your heart
Let no one steal your dreams
Let no one tell you that you can't
Let no one hold you back
Let no one tell you that you won't
Set your sights and keep them fixed
Set your sights on high
Let no one steal your dreams
Your only limit is the sky
Let no one steal your dreams
Follow your heart
Follow your soul
For only when you follow them
Will you feel truly whole
Set your sights and keep them fixed
Set your sights on high
Let no one steal your dreams
Your only limit is the sky

Paul Cookson

Radicalisation and Terrorism: A Teacher's Handbook for Addressing Extremism
© Alison Jamieson, Jane Flint and Brilliant Publications

STORYLINE: Bobo – a narrative of hate

The scene is a refugee camp with tents and tin huts in the (fictional) country of Exland. Bobo – a young boy aged 13 – is listening to his grandfather tell stories of when the family owned a farm with fertile land – a place where they could grow good crops and feed cattle. That was before soldiers from over the border in Wyland invaded Exland and drove the family off their farm. The Wylanders said that Exland had belonged to them two hundred years ago, and so they had a right to take it back. Grandfather, his son Jan, Jan's wife Rena and their two sons, Bobo and his brother Sam, are forced onto a truck with many others and driven for two days to a camp in another part of the country. This camp is close to a city and near a big industrial complex. Jan, Bobo's father, finds a job in a factory but he hates it. He misses the farm. Jan's employers don't respect their workers and treat them badly. Rena, Bobo's mother, has to work as cleaner for a family of rich Wylanders. She grows thin and her hair starts to grey, though she is still quite young. Every day grandfather talks about his hatred for the Wylanders, and his anger and hatred are passed down to Bobo and Sam. Once their family had their own home and they were strong and proud. Now they are hardly surviving.

Sam is 17. He has a job in a market garden, which is between the camp and the city, and to reach it he has to go through a Wyland army checkpoint and show a special pass. He is often searched and the guards enjoy being rude to him, saying insulting things about Exland. Because they are in charge, he cannot say anything, but it makes him furious inside. He feels humiliated, as if he counts for nothing and is being crushed into the ground under the heels of the soldiers. Through his work he makes new friends, then he starts to come home very late at night and gradually he stops going to work altogether. He has long conversations on his mobile phone but never tells his family what he is thinking or doing. One day he and a companion throw a homemade bomb at the army checkpoint. The bomb explodes and kills three soldiers, but Sam is killed in the blast as well.

Jan, Rena and Bobo leave the camp in a hurry, bundling grandfather into an old truck, and drive away as fast as possible, afraid of being killed by the soldiers. They manage to get to the coast and from there they take a boat to another country. Here Bobo goes to school and learns a new language, but he finds it hard to settle down or make friends. His life feels very strange, as if it is split in two. When he is at school he is in the new country, but when he is at home with his sad, angry parents, he feels he is back in Exland. Their TV sometimes shows news of Exland, which is still ruled by Wylanders. Life is hard for the Exlanders; they don't have enough to eat and are often treated badly. There have been protests, some of them violent, but they have been put down fiercely. Years pass and Bobo, who is clever at school but can't see any point in studying, gets a job at a building site.

One evening after work he meets two women from Exland who, like him, are exiles. One of them is skilled on the computer and has set up a website for people who left after the invasion. The website explains what happened, and shows how badly the Exlanders are being treated. It asks all the exiles to do something to help. The other woman is a very powerful speaker. When she talks at meetings, or even just to Bobo, he feels himself filling up with fire and fury. The women introduce him to other exiles and suddenly Bobo feels he belongs, he has found his identity. He identifies with this group of people who share his background and his feelings. They argue all the time about what they should do. Sending money is one possibility, but Bobo wants to be involved, he wants to act. He has a goal – he wants the Exlanders to have the right to live freely in their own country again. He wants to be responsible for taking his family home. The two women say that in order to achieve that goal he must go back and attack the Wylanders who occupy Exland. They warn Bobo he might get killed too, like his brother Sam, but he doesn't care. In fact it makes him want to go all the more. Nothing could be more noble than to die like Sam.

Before this time, Bobo had felt lost and without any direction for the future. The two women make him feel proud again, give his life a purpose. They arrange for him to go back secretly to Exland. He says nothing to his family but takes a plane and then a bus and slips across the border. A man is waiting to take him to a training camp in the mountains. There he joins a group of rebels and is given a gun. His companions are all from Exland too. They are hard, bitter men. They don't seem interested in freedom and peace, only in money, weapons and winning power for themselves. They want to kill as many Wylander settlers as possible; it doesn't matter if they are women and children. They sell drugs and steal cars – anything to get money and have more power over others in the group. Bobo's group is sent on a mission. They raid a farm

(Bobo wonders if it was his grandfather's) and kill everyone on it except a boy aged 10 – Bobo's age when he and his family were driven off their farm. The child is crying and alone. Bobo suddenly wonders what he is doing there. Where has all the hatred led him – just to kill a bunch of farm workers and this boy's family, leaving him alone in the world? An orphan who in turn will carry hatred around all his life. Was this family the enemy? Is violence bringing any good to anyone? Bobo thought he was fighting for a just cause, but now he feels that killing innocent people has turned him into a terrorist.

Bobo leaves his group and goes back across the border, taking the boy with him to his parents' house. They have been worried sick about him. They never imagined that he would go and fight; he always seemed a quiet, peaceful character. They are happy to have him back and to give the little boy a home. Bobo decides there must be a better way to fight than by killing ordinary people. With help and money from local community leaders, Bobo sets up a crafts market where Exlanders can use traditional skills to make products for the local community. The newspapers write about it. Local politicians are interested, and he hopes to speak to a member of the government. The government might then ask the leaders of Wyland to talk about a solution to the problem. Violence cannot be the answer. As Bobo has discovered, terrorism only creates more hatred and more violence.

Radicalisation and Terrorism: A Teacher's Handbook for Addressing Extremism
© Alison Jamieson, Jane Flint and Brilliant Publications
This page may be photocopied for use by the purchasing institution only.

School scenarios – Role-play cards

Dialogue	**Peaceful Protest**	**Violent protest**
Head teacher: reasonable, prepared to listen and approachable.	**Head teacher**: ready to listen but does not like change and has clear ideas of how he/she wants to run school.	**Head teacher**: has a bad temper, is unwilling to listen, and wants to run school his/her way. Does not like change.
Issue: pupils want to change the school uniform rule so that ties are not worn in hot summer months.	**Issue**: pupils want to have more PE/sports lessons each week. They have asked but head teacher says it is impossible for lack of money.	**Issue**: pupils are angry at the way the school is run. Their opinions are never listened to. They want to have more voice in school affairs. They want the head teacher to leave.
Pupils: believe in the right to have their voices heard. They ask for a meeting to discuss the issue. Head teacher agrees to this, and a discussion takes place.	**Pupils**: think decision is unfair as other schools have more sports lessons. They find out how other schools fund sports coaching and decide to organise a peaceful protest outside the school.	**Pupils**: a few 'hotheads' think that bold action is necessary to change things and to get the message across. They slash a tyre of the head teacher's car with a knife. He/she drives off and almost crashes car. Finds the cuts in the tyre.
Outcome: a compromise is found. Pupils arrive and leave school wearing ties but take them off in class.	**Outcome**: the pupils' protest is heard by parents and community leaders. They discuss matter with head teacher. Agreement is found when community leaders and parents together agree to share the cost of another sports teacher.	**Outcome**: discipline at the school becomes stricter. Guilty pupils are expelled from school.

If mice could roar

If mice could roar

And elephants soar

And trees grow up in the sky,

If tigers could dine

On biscuits and wine,

And the fattest of men could fly!

If pebbles could sing

And bells never ring

And teachers were lost in the post;

If a tortoise could run

And losses be won,

And bullies be buttered on toast;

If a song brought a shower,

And a gun grew a flower,

This world would be nicer than most!

Ruskin Bond

Glossary of Key Vocabulary

abolish: to get rid of

ally; allied: a friend or partner, often in a military sense; in a (military) partnership with

ambition: a goal, something to work very hard towards

amputate: cut off

assassin: someone who deliberately seeks out and kills a particular individual

audience: those who listen to or watch a performance

ban: to make something unlawful

bargain: an agreement between two or more people that involves promising to do something in exchange for something else

beacon: signal or sign that helps people to find their way

betray: to deceive, to be disloyal to, to help the enemies of

bias, biased: a preference or favour for one side rather than another; being in favour of one side rather than another

campaign: to work for a cause, or to work to make something happen

cause: a set of ideas or goals that people strongly believe in

cease-fire: an agreement, sometimes for a short time only, by both sides of a conflict to stop attacking one another

censorship: the refusal to allow something to be written or talked about

cherish: to hold dearly, to treasure

civil war: a war fought between rival groups of citizens within the same country

civilian: someone who is not a member of the armed forces

common ground: an area that people share, a place where they can agree

communication: a way of being in touch with people or sharing messages

compromise: an agreement where each side gives up a part of what it wants

consequences: the result or effects of something that has happened earlier

corrupt: to make someone dishonest or wicked

court: a place where legal cases are heard and decisions about justice are made; also a group of people who make legal decisions in a courtroom, for example a judge and jury

define: to give all the information about what something/someone is

definition: a way of describing exactly what something is

degenerate: to become worse

destructive: causing great damage and harm

dialect: a local or regional form of a main language

discrimination: the act of treating people differently for a reason (a reason which is in the mind of the person who discriminates)

dominate: to lead or be the strongest member of a group

domination: power over other people

equal rights: the same rights in law as other people

exile: someone who has felt it necessary to leave his/her native country and live abroad

extreme: something or someone that is very different, very strong, very far away, or very unusual compared to others

extremism: very strong views that not many people share, or that not many people think are acceptable or correct

fine: a sum of money that is paid as a punishment for breaking the law

gag: literally a piece of cloth that covers the mouth and prevents someone from speaking – here referring to something that prevents the media from speaking

general election: a vote to choose the people who will govern a country

grievance: a feeling of anger that a wrong has not been put right

harmony: peace, agreement, order (also a musical term)

hijack: to take control of a vehicle (bus, train, plane) by force

hostage: someone who is held prisoner by a person or group of people

humiliated: made to feel worthless and unimportant

hunger strike: a refusal to eat until a request or demand is met

ideal: (noun) the best outcome for the individual or group concerned

identify with: to see oneself as being similar to, or in the same situation as, someone else

identity: all the different parts of who a person is

intruder: someone who enters a building unlawfully, often to commit a crime

jihad: in faith terms, a struggle with one's duties, relationships and responsibilities; in a broader sense, a holy war or struggle on behalf of Islam

just cause: a set of reasons which are good or noble

justify: to try to show that something is right, to give good reasons for something

kidnap: to take and keep someone in a secret place against their will, usually for a ransom

live: something that we see happening at the exact moment that it happens

martyr: term used to describe someone who dies or is put to death because of a belief, principle or cause

mass media: means of communication, news and information such as newspapers, TV, radio and Internet that are open to very large numbers of people. Often shortened to media

massacre: the violent killing of a large number of people

mediator: someone who helps people to talk to each other when they disagree strongly about something

motto: a saying or slogan that contains a message

mouthpiece: a spokesperson, someone who represents the views of a person or group

movement: a group or groups of people who share the same goals (eg a peace movement)

negotiate: to make a bargain, find an agreement

negotiator: a person who makes a bargain or agreement

offender: someone who commits an offence or crime

overreact: to respond too strongly to something

patriotic: loyal, showing love for one's country

performance: a show or public display

petition: a letter to people in authority signed by several or many people

political power: the power to decide how things are done in a community

polluted: dirty or harmful to health

prejudice: feelings of dislike or hostility towards something or someone

prison sentence: a fixed time that someone must spend in prison after breaking the law

propaganda: information or ideas, usually exaggerated or misleading, to help a political cause

public opinion: a view held by a large section of the population

publicity: a high level of public attention

radical: very different, unusual or extreme

radicalisation: the process by which a person's views become extreme, especially with regard to support for or use of violence

ransom: a sum of money demanded for the freedom of a hostage

rebel: (noun) someone who fights against authority or the people in charge

reconciliation: a way of making peace, bringing people back together

recruit: to persuade someone to join a group or organisation

refugee: a person who leaves home as a result of war or other great difficulty and looks for help and safety in another place

Remembrance Day: a day when people remember those who have died as a result of war or conflict

restorative justice: justice that repairs the harm that has been done after a crime has been committed

revolution: a time of great change when a government is overturned and a new one takes over

sabotage: to deliberately damage something so that it does not work properly

sacrifice: a gift or offering of great value, usually as part of religious worship

suffrage: the right to vote

suppression: the putting down or holding back of something/someone

symbol: an example or picture that represents something

tradition: a custom or belief that is passed down through generations

truce: a stop or halt to fighting (usually lasting longer than a cease-fire)

Ubuntu: (from the Nguni group of African languages) a sense of belonging together, caring for one another

United Nations: an organisation set up in 1945 to which almost all countries belong

universal definition: a way of describing something that all countries can agree on

universal suffrage: the right to vote for all adults (usually persons over the age of 18)

Endnotes

Introduction
[1] Hooper, Simon: 'Sharp increase in under-18s "at risk" of being radicalised into jihadists', *The Independent*, 23 March 2014.
[2] HM Government: *Prevent Duty Guidance for England and Wales*, March 2015.
[3] The Quilliam Foundation (May 2014): *Jihad Trending: A Comprehensive Analysis of Online Extremism and How to Counter it* by Ghaffar Hussain and Dr Erin Marie Saltman, London.

How to Get the Most from this Handbook
[4] www.pshe-association.org.uk (2014): *Creating a PSHE Education Policy for your School*, PSHE Association.

Definitions, Terminology and Sources
[5] Davies, Lynn (2008): *Educating Against Extremism*, Trentham Books, Stoke on Trent.
[6] Hoffman, Bruce (2006): *Inside Terrorism*, Colombia University Press, New York, p 40.
[7] Gearty, Conor (1991): *Terror*, Faber & Faber, London, p 1.
[8] www.legislation.gov.uk/ukpga/2000/11/contents
[9] http://www.un.org/en/terrorism/instruments.shtml
[10] https://www.gov.uk/government/publications/prevent-strategy-2011
[11] Richardson, Louise (2007): *What Terrorists Want: Understanding the Terrorist Threat*, Random House, London, p 14.
[12] Horgan, John (2005): 'The social and psychological characteristics of terrorism and terrorists' in *Root Causes of Terrorism: Myths, Reality and Ways Forward* (ed. Tore Bjørgo), Routledge, Abingdon, p 45.
[13] Alderdice the Lord John, FRCPsych (2004): 'Understanding Terrorism – the Inner World and the Wider World', paper presented at a conference in London, 26 March 2004, to celebrate 70th anniversary of the Portman Clinic, subsequently published in June 2005 edition of the *British Journal of Psychotherapy*.
[14] Richardson, Louise (2007): *op cit*, p 14.
[15] Silke, Andrew (2005): 'Fire of Iolaus: the role of state countermeasures in causing terrorism and what needs to be done' in *Root Causes of Terrorism, op.cit*, pp 243–4.
[16] Jamieson, Alison (1989): *The Heart Attacked: Terrorism and Conflict in the Italian State*, Marion Boyars Publishers, London, p 271.
[17] 'MI5 report challenges views on terrorism in Britain', *The Guardian*, 20 August 2008.
[18] English, Richard (2009): *Terrorism, How to Respond*, Oxford University Press, Oxford, pp 33–34.
[19] Sen, Amartya (2006): *Identity & Violence. The Illusion of Destiny*, Penguin, London, p 165.
[20] Jamieson, Alison (January 1993): *Collaboration: New Legal and Judicial Procedures for Countering Terrorism*, Conflict Studies 257, Research Institute for the Study of Conflict and Terrorism, London.

Unit 1
[21] http://www.unicef.org/southafrica/SAF_resources_crcchildfriendly.pdf

Unit 2
[22] Lewis, Bernard (2003): *The Assassins, A Radical Sect in Islam*, Phoenix, London, p ix.
[23] Rosen, Andrew (1974): *Rise Up Women*, Routledge & Kegan Paul, London, p 188.
[24] http://www.1914-1918.net/faq.htm
[25] More information on the Suffragette movement can be found at: http://spartacus-educational.com/Wwspu.htm
[26] Mandela, Nelson (1995): *Long Walk to Freedom*, Abacus, London, p 438.

---

[27] Mandela, Nelson (1995): *op cit*, p 623.

[28] Larry King Live, CNN Television, 16 May 2000.

Unit 3

[29] This Storyline is fictional, but is inspired by an account from John Horgan (2009): *Walking Away from Terrorism: Accounts of Disengagement from Radical and Extremist Movements*, Routledge, London and New York, pp 63–76.

[30] Davies, Lynn (2008): *op cit*, pp 19–20.

[31] http://www.un.org/en/terrorism/instruments.shtml The UN conventions, the crimes they relate to and dates of signature are:

1. Unlawful acts aboard aircraft (1963)
2. Unlawful seizure of aircraft (1970)
3. Unlawful acts against the safety of civil aviation (1971)
4. Crime against internationally protected persons, including diplomatic agents (1973)
5. The taking of hostages (1979)
6. The protection of nuclear material (1980)
7. Unlawful acts of violence against airports (1988)
8. Unlawful acts against the safety of maritime navigation (1988)
9. Unlawful acts against the safety of fixed [oil or gas] platforms (1988)
10. The marking of plastic explosives for the purpose of detection (1991)
11. The suppression of terrorist bombings (1997)
12. The suppression of the financing of terrorism (1999)
13. The suppression of acts of nuclear terrorism (2005)
14. Unlawful acts against the safety of civil aviation (2010)

[32] Irshad Hussain, family friend of Mumtaz and Parween Tanweer, interviewed for article 'One day, seven lives, one year on', *The Independent*, 7 July 2006.

Unit 4

[33] Scieska, Jon (1991): *The True Story of the Three Little Pigs*, Picture Puffin, London.

[34] http://www.africanexecutive.com/modules/magazine/archives.php?magazine=563
The African Executive, Issue 50, 05–12 April 2006.

[35] Willow Wilson, G. (2014): *Ms. Marvel Volume 1: No Normal* Marvel–US, New York.

[36] http://blogs.lse.ac.uk/humanrights/2015/02/03/comics-and-human-rights-kamala-khan-and-the-narrative-of-terror/
According to a blog by PhD student Maria Werdine Norris, 'Kamala Khan disrupts the narrative that problematizes Muslims.... The book counters the relentlessly negative portrayal of Muslims in media and popular culture and its success make it clear that diversity matters.'

Unit 5

[37] For more on this project see http://www.commonwealth-of-nations.org/xstandard/Youth%20in%20the%20Commonwealth2010.pdf, pp 150–151.

[38] Obituary by Phil Davison, *Financial Times Weekend* 1–2 August 2009.

[39] In particular, Adriana Faranda, interviewed in Jamieson, Alison (1989): *op cit*.

[40] Alderdice, the Lord John, 'Rights, Respect and Reconciliation', talk presented at an international seminar on 'The Truth Commissions and the new challenges for the promotion of Human Rights' held at the Ministry of Foreign Affairs in Santiago, Chile, 11 April 2001.

[41] Truth and Reconciliation Commission: *Final Report*, Foreword Volume 6, 21 March 2003.

Bibliography and Further Reading

On terrorism:

Alderdice the Lord John, FRCPsych (2004): 'Understanding Terrorism – the Inner World and the Wider World', paper presented at a conference in London, 26 March 2004, to celebrate 70th anniversary of the Portman Clinic, subsequently published in June 2005 edition of the *British Journal of Psychotherapy*.

Commonwealth Secretariat (2007): *Civil Paths to Peace*. Report of the Commonwealth Commission on Respect and Understanding (chair, Amartya Sen), London.

Davies, Lynn (2008): *Educating Against Extremism*, Trentham Books, Stoke on Trent.

English, Richard (2009): *Terrorism, How to Respond*, Oxford University Press, Oxford.

Gearty, Conor (1991): *Terror*, Faber & Faber, London.

Gearty, Conor (2008): *Human Rights, Civil Society and the Challenge of Terrorism*. A Centre for the Study of Human Rights report, London School of Economics and Political Science.

Gearty, Conor (2013): *Liberty and Security*, Polity Press, Cambridge.

Hoffman, Bruce (2006): *Inside Terrorism*, Colombia University Press, New York.

Horgan, John (2005): 'The social and psychological characteristics of terrorism and terrorists' in *Root Causes of Terrorism: Myths, Reality and Ways Forward* (ed. Tore Bjørgo), Routledge, Abingdon.

Horgan, John (2009): *Walking Away from Terrorism: Accounts of Disengagement from Radical and Extremist Movements*, Routledge, London and New York.

Richardson, Louise (2007): *What Terrorists Want: Understanding the Terrorist Threat*, Random House, London.

Sen, Amartya (2006): *Identity & Violence. The Illusion of Destiny*, Penguin, London.

The Quilliam Foundation (May 2014): *Jihad Trending: A Comprehensive Analysis of Online Extremism and How to Counter it* by Ghaffar Hussain and Dr Erin Marie Saltman, London.

Other:

Bond, Ruskin (2007): *Ruskin Bond's Book of Verse*, Penguin Books India, New Delhi.

Mandela, Nelson (1995): *Long Walk to Freedom*, Abacus, London.

Tutu, Desmond (1999): *No Future without Forgiveness*, Rider books, London.

Suggested Online Resources

Overarching websites/background reading

https://www.gov.uk/government/publications/tackling-extremism-in-the-uk-report-by-the-extremism-taskforce
A policy which sets out practical proposals for tackling extremism in the UK. (4th December 2013)

https://www.gov.uk/
All current Government policies can be found on this website, including the *Prevent* strategy (2011)
https://www.gov.uk/government/publications/prevent-strategy-2011
Objective 3, subsection 10, pp 63–71, deals with the issues affecting schools and children.

http://rt.com/uk/207775-uk-police-extremism-schools/
Police teaching anti-extremism in schools as part of the Government's *Prevent* strategy. (November 2014)

https://www.mi5.gov.uk/home/about-us/what-we-do/the-threats/terrorism.html
Provides a brief explanation of what terrorist groups seek to achieve.

https://www.mi5.gov.uk/home/about-us/what-we-do/the-threats/terrorism/international-terrorism.html
Details of current terrorist groups and an assessment of the level of threat to the UK.

Websites for further resources, materials

http://globaldimension.org.uk/glp/page/10757
Global learning programme – recommended reading section is useful, as are several articles on teaching and discussing the Syrian conflict. This website suggests some teaching strategies which focus on developing analysis and critical thinking skills.

Excellent section on resources for teachers. Search results under the term 'Terrorism' brings recent attacks such as *Charlie Hebdo* into focus: http://globaldimension.org.uk/news/item/19939

On this website, further links to an American website:
https://www.extension.purdue.edu/purplewagon/EDUC-TEACHERS/MAINEduc-Teachers.htm
The website supports parents and teachers in discussing difficult issues such as terrorism and extremism.

http://www.citizenshipfoundation.org.uk/index.php
A website with a lot of resources on citizenship and provides links to the document: 'Teaching controversial issues in schools', online version: http://www.citizenshipfoundation.org.uk/main/page.php?92

http://www.oxfam.org.uk/education/resources
Up-to-date resources dealing with global issues and resources which could be used in the classroom.

http://www.oxfam.org.uk/education/whole-school
The Oxfam website provides teachers with a planning framework for global citizenship in the 21st century. There is also a guide specifically aimed at new teachers.

A useful website if you are looking for a whole school assembly, or year group assembly dealing with difficult issues. A recent example is an assembly providing a response to the terrorist attack in France against the staff of the satirical magazine *Charlie Hebdo*.

Acknowledgements

Alison is grateful to several distinguished scholars with whom she had the privilege of discussing the principal themes of this book. Particular thanks go to Professor Amartya Sen of Harvard University, the Lord Alderdice, FRCPsych, former Speaker of the Northern Ireland Assembly and one of the architects of the Northern Ireland peace process, Professor Conor Gearty of the London School of Economics, Professor Bruce Hoffman of Georgetown University and Professor John Horgan at the University of Massachusetts Lowell.

We owe a debt of gratitude to Narinder Gill, formerly Head teacher of Hunslet Moor Primary School in Beeston, Leeds, whose efforts in the school after the London bombings were a stimulus to our writing.

We thank Mr Ruskin Bond and his publishers, Penguin Books India, for their kind permission to reproduce 'If mice could roar'.

We thank Paul Cookson for his kind permission to reproduce 'Let no one steal your dreams'.

Thanks to Megan Wilkinson, the first 'guinea pig' of the questionnaire, then aged 11.

We are especially grateful to the team at Brilliant Publications for all the hard work of producing the book, and to Priscilla Hannaford for believing in us. A huge thank-you to our editor Marie Birkinshaw for her guidance and expertise. Any errors are, however, ours alone.

We would also like to thank friends and family members for discussions on the book and who encouraged us every step of the way, in particular husbands Nigel and Chris.

While the book is dedicated to the children who will be our future, our final tribute is to the much-loved brother and father Mike Frew, whom we lost in December 2014.

Biographical Notes

Alison Jamieson is an independent consultant and author who has written extensively in English and Italian on issues of political violence, organised crime and drugs. Her books include *The Heart Attacked: Terrorism and Conflict in the Italian State* (Marion Boyars, London, 1989); *The Antimafia: Italy's Fight against Organized Crime*, (Palgrave Press, Basingstoke/New York, 2000). She wrote two school texts on terrorism for Wayland publishers (UK) in 1991 and 1995 and a third, entitled *Can the War on Terrorism be Won?* for Arcturus/Franklin Watts, published in October 2008. Between 1992 and 1997 she was a regular guest lecturer at the NATO Defence College in Rome. She has worked as consultant to the United Nations Office on Drugs and Crime and to the International Narcotics Control Board, and was principal author of the first *UN World Drug Report* (Oxford University Press, Oxford, 1997). Her studies of Italian left-wing terrorism brought her into direct contact with victim families, lawyers and judges, as well as numerous terrorist group members, whom she interviewed in and outside prison, including those responsible for the kidnap and murder of former Italian prime minister Aldo Moro. For *The Antimafia* she interviewed judges, politicians, law enforcement officials, priests and social activists involved in combatting the Mafia after the 1992 murders of judges Giovanni Falcone and Paolo Borsellino, with whom she had talked at length.

Alison was born and educated in Scotland but has lived in Italy since 1984.

Jane Flint is a primary school teacher with 13 years' classroom experience. She was teaching in a school of predominantly Muslim children in the Beeston area of Leeds at the time of the London bombings in 2005. She was responsible for introducing inter-faith discussions into the classroom in Leeds and arranging for Muslim, Anglican and Sikh faith leaders to visit her classes. She worked as a volunteer in a girls' secondary school in Uganda in the summer of 2007. Jane devised the classroom activities; her teaching experiences informed and guided the text throughout.

COVENTRY COLLEGE LRC
City Campus